Published by PrepScholar

Cover design by Alex Heimbach

Table of Contents

Introduction to ACT Science

So you're struggling with ACT Science? Don't panic! The science section of the ACT is notoriously confusing and lots of students have a hard time figuring it out.

In this book, we lay out everything you need to know about the ACT science section and how you can best prepare, so you're completely ready for it on test day.

Who We Are (and Why You Should Trust Our Advice)

You might be wondering why PrepScholar, known for its online ACT prep program, is going old school and writing an ACT book. As ACT experts who have made it our mission to understand the test and help students succeed, we are dedicated to providing you with the best resources to achieve your academic and personal goals.

This book is based on our deep study of ACT Science and experience tutoring thousands of students. It will help you build a solid understanding of the test, as well as offering strategies that actually work.

If you're self-motivated, prep books can be a great way to learn content, practice strategies, and try sample questions.

However, if you're struggling to make progress studying on your own, consider checking out PrepScholar's online ACT program. Our prep program integrates the extensive info and expert advice in this book with added accountability features. We help you plan out and stick to your study schedule, keep track of your progress, and focus on the specific skills and practice problems that you most need to improve your scores.

How to Use This Book

In this guide, we cover every question type on the ACT Science section and give you strategies to attack them. In addition, we provide you with our best ACT Science tips and teach you how to get the most out of your ACT Science practice.

If you're serious about raising your ACT Science score, read through every chapter. By mastering all the key concepts, engaging with realistic practice questions, and reviewing your mistakes, you'll dramatically improve your ACT Science score.

We've organized the chapters based on how you'll proceed through your ACT Science prep. We'll start off by looking at the ACT at a high level and how to get yourself in the right mindset. Next, we'll dive into the individual skills tested on ACT Science and the different question types you'll see. Finally, we'll review key tips and explain how to avoid common mistakes.

Chapter 1: What's in the ACT Science Section?

You've taken many science exams in your school career, and you probably feel like you know what to expect from ACT Science.

However, for this test, there will be no long lists of scientific facts you need to memorize, no cycles or diagram to remember. Instead, you'll need to read passages of new scientific information filled with graphs and charts and be able to immediately understand that information so you can answer questions about it.

The questions are fast paced, cover a wide range of topics, and are often designed to trick you. Simply put, ACT Science is like no science test you've taken before.

Many students don't realize that the format of the ACT Science section is much more similar to the Reading section than the Math section. Each ACT Math question has its own task or problem. However, for both ACT Science and ACT Reading, the questions aren't individual; instead you'll read a passage, then answer a series of questions on that passage.

In this chapter, we dive into the formatting of ACT Science and explain the types of questions you'll see on this section, how you'll be graded, and how you can use this information to raise your ACT Science score.

Format and Timing of the ACT Science Section

The ACT Science section lasts 35 minutes and contains 40 questions. This gives you about 53 seconds to answer each question. There will be six or seven passages in the section, and the passages may contain graphs, charts, experiment summaries, and conflicting viewpoints from scientists. The passages may focus on a variety of areas such as biology, chemistry, physics, and earth/space sciences (including geology, astronomy, and meteorology).

Each passage is followed by four to seven questions. All questions on ACT Science are multiple choice with four answer choices. To do well on this section, you need to be able to quickly but accurately read and understand scientific data so you can answer the questions correctly in the time given.

Number of questions	40
Time limit	35 minutes
Approximate time per question	53 seconds
Question type	Multiple choice with four answer choices

ree Types of Passages You'll See

There are three main types of passages you'll see on ACT Science: Data Representation, Research Summaries, and Conflicting Viewpoints.

During the exam, you'll typically see two or three Data Representation passages, two or three Research Summaries passages, and one Conflicting Viewpoints passage.

For most ACT Science questions, you'll need to analyze data and experiments, though there will also be some questions that require you to compare conflicting viewpoints between scientists.

Below is a chart summarizing the different passages you'll see on ACT Science, and below that are descriptions and a sample question for each passage type.

Type of Passage	Skills Needed	Number of Questions (Percent of Questions)
Data Representation	Read and understand data	About 15 questions (35%)
Research Summaries	Interpret the design and results of experiments	About 18 questions (50%)
Conflicting Viewpoints	Compare, contrast, and analyze opposing viewpoints	About 7 questions (15%)

Data Representation

Data Representation passages present you with a short paragraph or two as well as one to four visual representations of data (such as graphs, tables, and/or scatterplots). Many passages will mention specific studies and label sections as Study 1/2/3.

For these questions, you'll need to read graphs, interpret scatterplots, and explain information presented in tables. While some background knowledge of the subject being tested can be helpful, it's more important that you are able to read and understand data.

Soils are composed of mixtures of differently sized particles. Soils can be classified by texture (the composition of the soil based on proportions of sand, silt, and clay particles) and porosity (percent of a soil's total volume composed of open space). Table 1 shows soil particle types with their typical diameters. A well sorted soil is composed of particles with low variation in diameter, while a poorly sorted soil is composed of particles with wide variation in diameter.

Table 1	
Particle Category	Particle Diameter (mm)
Gravel	> 2.0
Very Coarse Sand	1.1-2.0
Coarse Sand	0.6-1.0
Medium Sand	0.26-0.5
Fine Sand	0.14-0.25
Very Fine Sand	0.07-0.13
Silt	0.004-0.06
Clay	< 0.004

Study 1

A 500g sample a soil (Soil 1) was washed through a screen with 0.06mm holes to remove all clay and silt particles. The soil remaining on the screen was dried and weighed, then sifted through a series of screens with progressively smaller holes to separate particles of different categories. The particles collected for each category were then weighed. This procedure was repeated for samples of 4 other soils (Soils 2-5). Table 2 shows the results of this study.

Table 2					
	Weight (g) of Particles				
Particle Category	Soil 1	Soil 2	Soil 3	Soil 4	Soil 5
Gravel	0	0	0	0	36
Very Coarse Sand	0	132	0	0	54
Coarse Sand	0	241	0	0	197
Medium Sand	0	127	35	134	76
Fine Sand	14	0	136	245	36
Very Fine Sand	11	0	79	96	33

Study 2

A sample was taken from each of Soils 1-5 and dried by heating at 101°C for 24 hours, and was then weighed. Table 3 shows the calculated porosity and the void ratio (ratio of the volume of open space to the volume of solid material) of each soil sample.

Table 3		
Soil	Porosity (%)	Void Ratio
1	45	0.82
2	34	0.52
3	43	0.75
4	42	0.72
5	10	0.11

Soils with a lower void ratio hold less water when saturated than soils with a higher void ratio. Based on this information, which of the following soils in Study 2 would hold the least water when saturated?

A: Soil 1

B: Soil 3

C: Soil 4

D: Soil 5

This is a typical Data Representation question where you'll need to be able to read and interpret a chart to solve the problem.

For this question, we're trying to figure out which soil holds the least water when saturated. The question states that soils with lower void ratios hold less water when saturated, so that means were looking for the soil in Study 2 with the lowest void ratio. Looking at the chart, we can see that Soil 5 has the lowest void ratio, 0.11. This means that answer choice D is the correct answer.

Research Summaries

These passages look similar to the Data Representation passages in that they usually present you with a short paragraph or two plus visuals (graphs, tables, scatterplots, or images).

The difference is that Research Summaries passages focus on a specific experiment or small group of experiments. The passages will usually label sections as Experiment 1/2/3 and may mention a scientist or student who is conducting the experiment. There may also be an image of how the experiments are set up.

These questions require you to interpret the design and results of experiments. Again, specific content knowledge isn't as important as knowledge of the scientific method and data collection. Check out this example:

In a chemical reaction, the rate expresses the time for the products of the reaction to be generated from the reactants. In the following experiments, a student investigates how different factors affect the rate at which potassium permanganate ($KMnO_4$) is reduced to form manganese (II) ions, carbon dioxide and water after reacting with oxalic acid ($H_2C_2O_4$). As $KMnO_4$ undergoes this reaction it changes in color from purple, to an orange-brown color, and eventually becomes colorless when the reaction is complete.

Experiment 1

A student mixed 15 mL of 1.0 M (moles/liter) $H_2C_2O_4$ in solution with 30 mL sulphuric acid and 60 mL water in a 250 mL beaker. In a separate 100 mL beaker, 15 mL of 0.1 M $KMnO_4$ solution was added. Prior to undergoing any reaction, $KMnO_4$ in solution is purple in color. The two beakers were cooled down to 0°C in an ice bath. The solution of KMnO4 was then added to the second beaker of $H_2C_2O_4$ and sulphuric acid. The time that it took the combined solutions to change color from purple to colorless was recorded. The same protocol was repeated at room temperature (25°) and after warming up both solutions in a water bath of 40°C and 50°C. The results are represented in Table 1.

Table 1

Trial	Temperature (°C)	Reaction Time (sec)
1	0	900
2	25	150
3	40	60
4	50	30

Experiment 2

The same protocol in Experiment 1 was repeated identically, except for that this time a single crystal of manganese sulphate ($KMnO_4$) was added to the solution of $KMnO_4$ prior to mixing with the solution of $H_2C_2O_4$ and sulphuric acid. In this reaction $MnSO_4$ serves as a catalyst. A catalyst is a compound that increases the rate of a reaction but is not consumed in the process. The results from Experiment 2 are shown in Table 2.

Table 2

Trial	Temperature (°C)	Reaction Time (sec)
5	0	282
6	25	52
7	40	28
8	50	14

Experiment 3

Once again the procedure followed in Experiment 1 was repeated, but this time all reactions occurred at room temperature (25°C). In each trial, the concentration of the $H_2C_2O_4$ used varied. The results from Experiment 3 are shown in Table 3.

Table 3

Trial	Concentration of $H_2C_2O_4$ (M)	Reaction Time (sec)
9	0.10	755
10	0.25	541
11	0.50	332
12	0.75	229

The influence of the following factors were investigated in the experiments with the exception of:

A: changing the concentration of $H_2C_2O_4$.

B: varying the temperature of the reaction.

C: changing the reaction vessel.

D: adding a catalyst to the reaction.

As you can see, compared to the Data Representation question, this question focuses more on understanding the experiments discussed in the passage as opposed to interpreting data in graphs and charts.

This question wants to know which of the following factors was NOT investigated in the experiment, so let's go through the answer choices one by one. We know that the concentration of $H_2C_2O_4$ was changed in Experiment 3, so A is incorrect. Temperature was varied in both Experiments 1 and 2 so B is incorrect. For answer choice D, there was a catalyst added to the reaction (the crystal of manganese sulphate added in Experiment 2), so that's out. In Experiment 1, it was mentioned that the reaction vessel was a 250 mL glass beaker. The vessel is not mentioned again, and it's stated that Experiment 2 and Experiment 3 were conducted the same way Experiment 1 was, except for explicitly mentioned changes. If something isn't mentioned again in subsequent experiments, that means it stayed the same for all experiments. Therefore, the reaction vessel was the only factor that wasn't investigated in the experiments, making C the correct answer.

Conflicting Viewpoints

Conflicting Viewpoints passages are the most different from the other passage types. These passages present you with two or more short essays that represent conflicting scientific viewpoints or theories.

You'll be tested on your ability to understand, analyze, and compare alternate viewpoints or hypotheses. Questions for these passages will center around a single situation or problem, and you will read two different viewpoints and compare the similarities and differences.

Here's an example:

In Cycas revoluta (a species of seed plant), males have cones that produce pollen, and females have cones that produce seeds. Pollination requires the movement of pollen from inside a male cone to inside a female cone, where multiple ovules are located and pollinated. The ovules then develop into seeds. Below, two students discuss this pollination process.

Experiments

The students proposed 3 experiments using a Cycas revoluta population in an area with sap beetles and in which the percentage of ovule pollination in normally 99% (see table).

Experiment	Procedure
1	Some female *Cycas revoluta* cones are covered with plastic bags that exclude insects and wind.
2	Some female *Cycas revoluta* cones are covered with mesh bags that exclude insects, but not wind.
3	Some female *Cycas revoluta* cones are covered with cylinders that exclude wind, but not insects.

Student 1

In Cycas revoluta, 80% of ovule pollination results from insect pollination, and 20% results from wind pollination. These are the only two pollination mechanisms.

Cycas revoluta have mutually beneficial relationships with certain species of insects. Sap beetles swarm male Cycas revoluta cones when these cones are releasing pollen. When they enter the cones, the sap beetles become covered with the plant's pollen. The sap beetles then visit the female Cycas revoluta cones and deposit some of the pollen when it rubs off them. In the absence of sap beetles, the percent of ovule pollination in Cycas revoluta is about 20%.

Wind pollination is infrequent because Cycas revoluta pollen is large and heavy, making it difficult for it to travel long distances by wind. Additionally, the openings in the female cones are aligned horizontally, so wind-borne pollen must be blown horizontally in order to enter these cones.

Student 2

Wind pollination causes the majority, about 90%, of Cycas revoluta pollination, while only about 10% of ovule pollination in Cycas revoluta is caused by insects. Without wind pollination, the percent of ovule pollination decreases by 90%. If neither of these processes occur, the percent of ovule pollination decreases by 100%.

Wind tunnel experiments show that the shape of the female Cycas revoluta cones creates air currents that facilitate the horizontal movement of pollen into these cones so it is easier for windborne pollen to enter. Additionally, male Cycas revoluta cones produce enormous quantities of pollen, a trait that is common only in wind-pollinated plants. This means the majority of pollen can miss the female cones and the cones will still be pollinated because so much pollen is carried by the wind.

Pollination by sap beetles is infrequent because the beetles prefer other plant species over Cycas revoluta and only rarely visit Cycas revoluta, minimizing the amount of pollination they can perform.

Suppose an experiment was conducted using a natural population of Cycas revoluta with all the male cones covered in plastic bags that blocked them from both wind and insects. Assuming that Student 1's hypothesis is correct, the percent of ovule pollination would be closest to:

A: 0%

B: 20%

C: 65 %

D: 95%

You can see that this passage differs significantly from the previous two, since it has only one visual and focuses mostly on the different opinions of the two students.

For this question, Student 1 states in the first paragraph that they believe wind and insect pollination are the only ways Cycas revoluta cones can be pollinated. If the male cones are blocked from distributing pollen by either of these methods, and assuming Student 1's hypothesis is correct, there would be no pollination, so the correct answer is A.

Scoring on the ACT Science Section

For each of the 40 questions on ACT Science, you'll receive one point if you get the question right, and zero points if you get the question wrong. You don't lose any points for incorrect answers, so you should make sure to answer every question.

The points you earn on ACT Science are then added together to make your raw score, which is out of 40. For example, if you answered 27 questions correctly, your raw score for ACT Science would be 27.

Your raw score is then converted to a scaled score between 1 and 36, which is the score you'll see when you get your exam results. The ACT uses scaled scores to make sure scores are consistent across multiple test dates. For example, they need to make sure a 28 on an October ACT represents the same level of skill as a 28 on an April ACT.

Why Does This Information Matter?

In order to do well on ACT Science, you need to know exactly what to expect in the section, from the types of passages you'll be seeing to exactly how quickly you need to answer each question. Knowing these types of details will make you more prepared for the exam, which can help you feel more confident and less anxious

If you know the format of ACT Science, you'll also be able to figure which parts of the science section you need to work on so you can strengthen these weaknesses well before exam day. Knowing the ACT Science well will help you notice the tricks test makers like to use on this section, so you aren't fooled by them. We'll go over these tricks in later chapters, but knowing the basic format of the section will make it easier to recognize them.

Additionally, you'll be able to answer questions much more quickly because you'll be used to how they're worded and the kind of information they'll be asking about. Time management is a key part of doing well on the ACT, and the faster you can accurately answer questions, the better your chance of getting a great score.

Chapter 2: The Key to Understanding ACT Science

Why is the ACT Science section so scary? Many students, even those who aced their science classes in school, find ACT Science to be the most challenging section of the exam. They don't understand the difficult science terms, they struggle to finish the section in time, they're overwhelmed by the amount of information in the tables and graphs, and the section just isn't how they expected it to be.

In fact, ACT Science is unlike any other science test you've taken, and that can make it intimidating.

How do you avoid being unprepared? By knowing the critical secret to ACT Science: you actually don't need to know much about science to do well. Instead, you need to be able to have strong critical reading skills - this is the fundamental basis for ACT Science!

In this chapter, we give an overview of the ACT Science section and explain the mindset you need to ace it.

Wait, ACT Science Doesn't Test Science?

While you might think the ACT Science section would test high-level science knowledge, you will be tested on very little actual science knowledge. Only about four questions out of the 40 rely on outside science knowledge. What you actually need to succeed on ACT Science is...reading skills!

The ACT is a nationwide test, administered to over a million students each year. Every student takes different science classes at different levels. It wouldn't be fair for the ACT to ask questions on, say, the nitrogen cycle or stoichiometry or thermodynamics because many students may not have studied those subjects in their science classes and would be at an immediate disadvantage compared to students who had studied them.

Additionally, even if the ACT could somehow create a science section that only covered topics every high school student in America had studied, the content to study would be enormous. You could have aced all your biology, chemistry, physics, and earth science classes and still do poorly on the science section if you were expected to remember things like what the different parts of the brain are called or what Kepler's three laws of planetary motion are.

It'd be like studying for multiple AP exams, and it's just too much information to learn and remember for just a single section of the ACT.

ACT Science needs to offer a level playing field that doesn't require students to spend dozens of hours trying to memorize varied facts and laws from across of all science. In order to do this, ACT Science focuses on testing basic science skills rather than specific knowledge.

The Key to Acing ACT Science

Since ACT Science tests only basic science skills, it ends up looking more like a reading test rather than a test you see in your science classes. In fact, it may help if you think of ACT Science as ACT Reading section #2 ,where you just happen to be reading about science experiments or studies.

If ACT Science is really more like a reading test with some extra graphs and charts added, what skills do you need to do well on it? Your reading comprehension skills will be key. All the information you need to answer the ACT Science questions is in the passages; but you need to know how to find it quickly and accurately.

You'll also need to be able to understand visuals like graphs and charts in order to answer questions on them, but you won't be expected to understand complex science experiments or terms.

Look at this sample passage and question which we saw in Chapter 1:

In a chemical reaction, the rate expresses the time for the products of the reaction to be generated from the reactants. In the following experiments, a student investigates how different factors affect the rate at which potassium permanganate ($KMnO_4$) is reduced to form manganese (II) ions, carbon dioxide and water after reacting with oxalic acid ($H_2C_2O_4$). As $KMnO_4$ undergoes this reaction it changes in color from purple, to an orange-brown color, and eventually becomes colorless when the reaction is complete.

Experiment 1

A student mixed 15 mL of 1.0 M (moles/liter) $H_2C_2O_4$ in solution with 30 mL sulphuric acid and 60 mL water in a 250 mL beaker. In a separate 100 mL beaker, 15 mL of 0.1 M $KMnO_4$ solution was added. Prior to undergoing any reaction, $KMnO_4$ in solution is purple in color. The two beakers were cooled down to 0°C in an ice bath. The solution of $KMnO_4$ was then added to the second beaker of $H_2C_2O_4$ and sulphuric acid. The time that it took the combined solutions to change color from purple to colorless was recorded. The same protocol was repeated at room temperature (25°) and after warming up both solutions in a water bath of 40°C and 50°C. The results are represented in Table 1.

Table 1

Trial	Temperature (°C)	Reaction Time (sec)
1	0	900
2	25	150
3	40	60
4	50	30

Experiment 2

The same protocol in Experiment 1 was repeated identically, except for that this time a single crystal of manganese sulphate ($KMnO_4$) was added to the solution of $KMnO_4$ prior to mixing with the solution of $H_2C_2O_4$ and sulphuric acid. In this reaction $MnSO_4$ serves as a catalyst. A catalyst is a compound that increases the rate of a reaction but is not consumed in the process. The results from Experiment 2 are shown in Table 2.

Table 2

Trial	Temperature (°C)	Reaction Time (sec)
5	0	282
6	25	52
7	40	28
8	50	14

Experiment 3

The procedure followed in Experiment 1 was repeated, but all reactions occurred at room temperature (25°C). In each trial, the concentration of $H_2C_2O_4$ varied. The results of Experiment 3 are shown in Table 3.

Table 3

Trial	Concentration of $H_2C_2O_4$ (M)	Reaction Time (sec)
9	0.10	755
10	0.25	541
11	0.50	332
12	0.75	229

The influence of the following factors were investigated in the experiments with the exception of:

A: changing the concentration of $H_2C_2O_4$.

B: varying the temperature of the reaction.

C: changing the reaction vessel.

D: adding a catalyst to the reaction.

There are a multiple scientific terms in the answer choices, but you don't need to use any science skills to answer the question; you just need to have strong reading skills. This question is worded in a somewhat overly complicated way, but it just wants to know which of the answer choices scientists didn't study in the experiment. Anything the scientists changed in the experiments was something they studied, so we're looking for the factor that remained the same for each of the three experiments.

Let's go through the answer choices one by one. By looking at Table 3, we know that the concentration of $H_2C_2O_4$ was changed in Experiment 3, so A is incorrect. Temperature was varied in both Experiments 1 and 2 so B is incorrect. Even if you don't know what a catalyst is, it's mentioned that a crystal of manganese sulphate was added in Experiment 2, so we know D is also incorrect.

In Experiment 1, it was mentioned that the reaction vessel was a 250 mL glass beaker. The vessel isn't mentioned again, and it's stated in the passage that Experiment 2 and Experiment 3 were conducted the same way Experiment 1 was, except for explicitly mentioned changes. If something isn't mentioned again in subsequent experiments, that means it stayed the same for all experiments. Therefore, the reaction vessel was the only factor that wasn't investigated in the experiments, making C the correct answer. We solved that question without any scientific analysis, but just by reading through the passage and accompanying figures and finding the information we needed.

Here are the three passage types you'll see on ACT Science as well as the skills needed to answer their associated questions:

- Data Representation Passages: These passages describe a study and are heavy on graphs and charts. You'll need to be able to read graphs, interpret trends, and calculate values.
- Research Summaries Passages: They describe an experiment that has multiple parts. For these you'll need to be able to understand experimental design, understand hypothetical experimental changes, and interpret experiments.
- Conflicting Viewpoints Passages: These passages will be structured around the opinions of two or more scientists who disagree on different parts of an experiment and its results. You'll need to understand and compare different viewpoints.

Answering these questions requires strong reading skills (to understand and compare viewpoints, interpret experiments, and understand hypothetical changes) and the ability to analyze data (to read graphs, interpret trends, and calculate values).

Don't Let the Science Terms Intimidate You

If ACT Science is more about reading, does that mean you need to understand every word in this section? Not at all. On nearly every ACT Science passage, you'll see at least one scientific vocab word you don't know or can't quite remember. Don't panic! Remember, you don't need to know high-level science to ace the science section.

Most of the time, the ACT simply adds those long, confusing vocab words to make a passage seem more complicated and to try to trip up students. However, on closer reading, you'll realize you don't need to understand nearly any of the vocab words to answer the question correctly. On the rare occasions that you need to understand a certain challenging vocab word to answer the problem, the passage will explain what the word means. In all other cases, don't stress yourself out trying to remember if you ever learned about the vocab term in class or while studying.

Here's what that looks like in a sample question:

Permeability is a measure of how fast water moves through a soil. It is known that permeability increases as the proportion, by weight, of a soil's particles that are coarse sand size or larger increases. Based on the results of Study 1 and Study 2, a soil with a large permeability likely has:

A: A high porosity and a large void ratio

B: A high porosity and a small void ratio

C: A low porosity and a large void ratio

D: A low porosity and a small void ratio

This question is asking about permeability, and if you aren't sure what permeability is, that's OK. The test writers define it right in the question: permeability measures how fast water moves through soil. Many students might know what permeability is, but others likely won't. ACT Science isn't designed to test your vocabulary skills; it's meant to test your ability to correctly read and analyze passages and accompanying figures.

So how should you tackle scientific vocabulary on the ACT? Think of it like a matching game. If you see a word you don't know in the passage or a question, find that same term in one of the visuals that accompany the passage.

Try this sample question:

Study 2

A sample was taken from each of Soils 1-5 and dried by heating at 101°C for 24 hours, and was then weighed. Table 3 shows the calculated porosity and the void ratio (ratio of the volume of open space to the volume of solid material) of each soil sample.

Table 3		
Soil	Porosity (%)	Void Ratio
1	45	0.82
2	34	0.52
3	43	0.75
4	42	0.72
5	10	0.11

Based on Table 3, another soil sample that had a void ratio of 0.79 would have had a corresponding porosity of:

A: Less than 10%

B: Between 10% and 42%

C: Between 43% and 45%

D: Greater than 45%

When you read this question, you may not know what void ratio or porosity is, but you actually don't need to know either definition. The question is asking what the porosity of a soil with a void ratio of 0.79 would be. Don't worry about figuring out what the vocab means, just find where void porosity is mentioned in Table 3. Void porosity is the right-hand column, and porosity is the middle column.

There are no soil samples with a void ratio of exactly 0.79, but there are samples with void ratios of 0.75 and 0.82, and they have porosities of 43% and 45%, respectively. Since 0.79 is in the middle of those two void ratios, it stands to reason that the porosity of the soil in question would be in the middle of those two porosities as well, so the correct answer is C.

As you just saw, this problem and many others on ACT Science can easily be solved without spending time trying to define and understand all the vocab you see. You just need to know how to find the correct information in the passage and the figures.

How Will Knowing What ACT Science Actually Tests Help You?

A major reason students struggle so much on ACT Science is because they think it will be like the science tests they took in school. This means they study the wrong information and are surprised come exam day when they're tested on information and skills that are completely different than what they expect.

You likely already know most of the skills ACT Science tests you on because they're fairly basic. However, in order to do well on ACT Science, you need to know exactly what to expect from this section, and that means understanding that this section is more like a reading exam than a science exam. In the following chapters, we'll discuss in detail the types of questions you'll see, what you'll be tested on, and exactly how you can prepare for ACT Science.

Chapter 3: Time Management on ACT Science

You can be a science genius, but if you can't answer the questions on ACT Science quickly enough, you won't get a high score. Running out of time is a very common problem on ACT Science. It's a fast-paced section, and it comes at the end of a long test that has probably already tired you out.

While many students put in significant time studying content and question types they struggle with, fewer spend time improving their time management skills, even though these can have just as big an impact on your final score. In this chapter, we go over timing strategies to use during the science section and tips to follow to make sure you're using your time effectively.

Overall Timing Strategy for ACT Science

As a reminder, you'll have 35 minutes to complete ACT Science, and there will be six to seven passages in the section, each followed by four to seven questions. This means you'll want to spend, on average, about five minutes on each passage, including reading the passage and answering each of the questions that follows it. However, don't take this as hard and fast rule. Some passages are longer or have more questions than others, but it's good to have a rough idea of how much time to spend on each passage so you don't get behind.

During the exam, check the clock every few questions to make sure you're on track with your timing. Some students find it helpful to write out when they should be finishing each passage to make sure they're on schedule. For example, if you start the science section at 11:00AM, you'll want to finish passage one at 11:05, passage two at 11:10, etc.

We also recommend saving the Conflicting Viewpoints passage for last, even if it occurs first or somewhere in the middle of the section. The Conflicting Viewpoints passage includes two short essays that have differing viewpoints. You'll need to read both essays completely to answer the questions. The Conflicting Viewpoints Passage doesn't include any visuals and requires an entirely different strategy and way of thinking, so it can break you out of your focused mindset if you tackle it in the middle of the section. It's also the longest passage, so try to save at least five minutes for it so you have time to read it through and then attempt the questions.

If you're really struggling with finishing the ACT Science section in time, and you're not aiming for a science score of 30 or above, you may want to consider skipping a passage so you have more time to focus on the rest of the questions. On average, to get a

26 on ACT Science, you only need to answer 30 out of the 40 questions correctly. This means you can completely skip an entire passage, get a few questions wrong on the other passages, and still get a 26. Skipping a passage isn't a good strategy if you want a top science score, but if you're aiming for a score somewhere in the 20s, skipping a passage can actually raise your score because you'll have more time to focus on the rest of the questions (about seven minutes per passage or 70 seconds per question).

The Biggest Timing Mistake: Don't Let Yourself Get Stuck on a Question

The most common timing mistake students make is letting themselves getting bogged down on one or two ACT Science questions and rushing through the rest of the section as a result. This can have disastrous effects on your score if you end up missing an entire passage or more, so don't let this happen to you.

What should you do if you find yourself stuck on a question? First, always keep track of your timing and how much time you have left. You should never let yourself spend more than 90 seconds on any question or more than seven to eight minutes on any passage. Doing so can cause you to need to skip multiple questions further on in the section, which will hurt your score. Ideally, you should spend exactly 52.5 seconds on each question in order to finish the section in time. However, you also need to account for time spent reading the passage and analyzing the visuals, not to mention the fact that you'll be able to answer some questions more quickly than others.

If you haven't been able to solve a problem in about 50 seconds, use process of elimination. Try to get rid of all the answer choices you know are wrong. Then, pick your favorite answer choice among what is left over. Even if you're not 100% sure, choose an answer anyway, and put a small star next to it so you can go back to it if you have time.

There are several reasons students commonly get stuck on an ACT Science question.

#1: You get overwhelmed by the visuals or numbers: There's a lot of information included in each ACT Science passage, and it's easy to get confused, especially because you need to analyze the data very quickly to keep moving through the section. Sometimes students will read a description or a graph that they just don't understand, and that can cause them to panic and think that, because they don't understand this piece of information, they won't be able to answer any questions on the passage, and they'll ruin their ACT Science score, which will ruin their entire ACT score, etc. Don't let yourself fall into this train of thought. Read through the questions so you know which pieces of information you need and which are irrelevant. Write your own notes in the margins to help you stay focused. If you're not entirely confident about your ability to analyze graphs or tables, we explain how to do this later on in the book.

#2: You spend too much time trying to understand the experiment or visuals: Many students waste time trying to understand all the graphs, tables, and data a passage includes before they even begin answering questions. Remember, the ACT will often add a lot of unnecessary information to make a problem seem more challenging and to try to trick you. Don't let yourself fall for this! Skim through the visuals and focus only on the main point they're making. Most of the information they include isn't needed for answering any of the questions (we discuss the best way to skim passages in the next section). You may find it easier to focus your attention by reading the questions first, figuring out exactly what you need to answer the question, and then going back and looking for only that information.

#3: You want to be 100% certain of your answer: When you're trying to maximize your ACT score it can be tempting to make absolutely sure you chose the correct answer before moving on to the next question. However, this double-checking can actually hurt your score by putting you behind schedule and causing you to miss later questions. Once you solve a particular problem, spend a few seconds, at most, making sure you haven't made any obvious errors, then move on to the next question. If you have time at the end of the section, you can always check your answers again, but you don't have the time to do this in the middle of the exam.

How to Skim Passages and Still Get the Key Information

We mentioned in the previous section how skimming passages can save you tons of time on ACT Science since you aren't getting bogged down by unimportant details. However, you need to know the correct way to skim science passages so that you're still getting the information you need to answer the questions.

Here's a sample passage that you've seen in previous chapters, but now we're going to show you how you should actually be reading it. We've included our skimming notes so you can see what information we found important and what information we skipped over.

In a chemical reaction, the rate expresses the time for the products of the reaction to be generated from the reactants. In the following experiments, a student investigates how different factors affect the rate at which potassium permanganate ($KMnO_4$) is reduced to form manganese (II) ions, carbon dioxide and water after reacting with oxalic acid ($H_2C_2O_4$). As $KMnO_4$ undergoes this reaction it changes in color from purple, to an orange-brown color, and eventually becomes colorless when the reaction is complete.

Notes: rate = how fast reactants turn into products in a reaction. These experiments studied how fast $KMnO_4$ became $H_2C_2O_4$.

During the reaction the solution goes from purple to colorless. We're not worrying about any of the alternative names or what the other products of the reaction are.

Experiment 1

A student mixed 15 mL of 1.0 M (moles/liter) $H_2C_2O_4$ in solution with 30 mL sulphuric acid and 60 mL water in a 250 mL beaker. In a separate 100 mL beaker, 15 mL of 0.1 M $KMnO_4$ solution was added. Prior to undergoing any reaction, $KMnO_4$ in solution is purple in color. The two beakers were cooled down to 0°C in an ice bath. The solution of $KMnO_4$ was then added to the second beaker of $H_2C_2O_4$ and sulphuric acid. The time that it took the combined solutions to change color from purple to colorless was recorded. The same protocol was repeated at room temperature (25°) and after warming up both solutions in a water bath of 40°C and 50°C. The results are represented in Table 1.

Table 1

Trial	Temperature (°C)	Reaction Time (sec)
1	0	900
2	25	150
3	40	60
4	50	30

Notes: There are solutions of $H_2C_2O_4$ and $KMnO_4$ that are mixed together. All the details of how much of each solution and the size of the beakers they were put in are irrelevant. When the solution becomes colorless, the reaction has stopped. This experiment was done at different temperatures. Table 1 shows how temperature affects reaction time. Reaction time decreases as temperature increases.

Experiment 2

The same protocol in Experiment 1 was repeated identically, except for that this time a single crystal of manganese sulphate ($KMnO_4$) was added to the solution of $KMnO_4$ prior to mixing with the solution of $H_2C_2O_4$ and sulphuric acid. In this reaction $MnSO_4$ serves as a catalyst. A catalyst is a compound that increases the rate of a reaction but is not consumed in the process. The results from Experiment 2 are shown in Table 2.

Table 2

Trial	Temperature (°C)	Reaction Time (sec)
5	0	282
6	25	52
7	40	28
8	50	14

Notes: The same experiment was done, but this time $KMnO_4$ was added which sped up the reaction time.

Experiment 3

Once again the procedure followed in Experiment 1 was repeated, but this time all reactions occurred at room temperature (25°C). In each trial, the concentration of the $H_2C_2O_4$ used varied. The results from Experiment 3 are shown in Table 3.

Table 3

Trial	Concentration of $H_2C_2O_4$ (M)	Reaction Time (sec)
9	0.10	755
10	0.25	541
11	0.50	332
12	0.75	229

Notes: The reaction was done again, but this time the temperature stayed the same and the concentration of $H_2C_2O_4$ changed. The columns in Table 3 are slightly different than those in Tables 1 and 2. As the concentration of $H_2C_2O_4$ increased, reaction time decreased.

By skimming the passage, we were able to get all the important information without getting bogged down in irrelevant details. For most ACT Science passages, the majority of the text will actually be useless in answering the questions. If you see a string of numbers/terms like the paragraph under "Experiment 1" that's a nearly surefire way that the ACT is just dumping useless information on you. They're trying to trick students by slowing them down and making them think they need to understand and remember all that data. However, only a small amount of the information in that paragraph was important.

When you're reading passages, always try to figure out the main point of an experiment or figure. For Experiment 1, it doesn't matter what size beaker was used or how much water was added; that's not the point of the experiment. The point of the experiment was seeing how different temperatures affect reaction time. That's the information you need to pay attention to when skimming.

Other Time Saving Tips for ACT Science

There are other tips you can follow to move more quickly through the science section. These are all easy to follow, but they can help you save significant time on the exam.

#1: Do Not Read the Instructions

You were probably taught to always read instructions, but do not read them on the day of the ACT. If you've taken ACT Science practice tests before, you know what's coming, and reading the instructions will only waste your limited testing time.

Here are the instructions, read them now and then never again:

"DIRECTIONS: There are several passages in this test. Each passage is followed by several questions. After reading a passage, choose the best answer to each question and fill in the corresponding oval on your answer document. You may refer to the passages as often as necessary. You are NOT permitted to use a calculator on this test."

Not very helpful, right? The instructions never change; so don't bother reading them on exam day.

#2: Decide on a Reading Method Beforehand

Well before exam day you should know which reading method works better for you: reading through the passage first and then answering questions, or reading through the questions first then looking through the passage for the information they ask for. One method isn't better than the other; it's all about which one you feel more comfortable with and gets you a higher score. This is one of the reasons why taking practice tests is so important, so you can learn which method works better for you. It's likely that you'll work faster using one method compared to the other, and knowing this will help you save time during the science section. (Note that for the Conflicting Viewpoints passage, it's best to read the two essays first before answering the questions, regardless of your reading method for the other passages.)

#3: Bubble in the Blanks at the End
We recommend marking your answers in your test booklet as you go work through the ACT Science section and only going back to bubble in the correct answers on your Scantron in the last minute or two of the exam. This will save you a bit of time, and every second really does count on ACT Science. There's no penalty for guessing on the ACT, so don't leave any blanks, even if you aren't sure of an answer. Every additional question or two that you answer correctly raises your score about one point, especially in the 30-36 range. There is no best letter to guess (even if you have heard C is the most used). All letters are used randomly and equally, so just pick your favorite letter and use it to answer all the questions you couldn't solve.

#4: Keep Your Energy Up
The ACT Science section is always the last section of the test. You'll be tired. You'll have already been sitting for over an hour and a half. Your wrist will hurt from writing, and your back will

hurt from sitting. You'll be wondering if you answered that math problem correctly.

You must let go of what happened on the last three sections of the test and stay focused the questions in front of you. There are several ways to stay energized and focused. First, take advantage of the breaks you get earlier in the exam. Get up and walk around, even if you don't really feel like it. Also, bring some snacks to eat at the break for an energy boost. Well before test day, you should also be used to completing an entire ACT in one sitting. The best way to do this is to take at least three full-length practice ACTs. Even if the science section is the section you want to focus most of your studying on, don't only take practice science sections. You need to understand how your mind and body will feel after testing for several hours so you can see how this affects you on the science section and be prepared for it.

Why Is Time Management Important?

Knowing how to manage time on ACT Science is just as important to getting a high score as knowing the content and skills you'll be tested on. Many students lose points because they aren't able to answer questions quickly enough.

Missing questions because of time management can be even more frustrating than missing them because you didn't know the answer. You would have gotten them right if you'd just had more time.

Fortunately, there are many ways to improve your time management skills, and as you figure out which methods work best for you and implement these strategies on practice tests, you'll be well prepared on test day.

Chapter 4: Reading Charts and Graphs

Many students are surprised by how many graphs and charts the ACT Science section contains. If you don't understand how to read figures like these, it will be basically impossible to do well on this section. The majority of ACT Science questions will ask you to find or analyze information from figures and tables, so these are definitely skills you need to feel confident about.

This chapter explains everything you need to be looking for when you look at a graph or chart (and the information you can ignore), shows the different types of graphs and charts you'll see on ACT Science, and works through numerous sample problems so you can see how you should use the information you see in figures to solve science questions.

The Core Elements of a Graph

We'll start off by reviewing the basic components of graphs and how to interpret them. This is basic information that you likely already know, but be sure to read this section anyway. The ACT often tests this information in ways different from how your math and science classes test them in school.

Labels

Labels are key to the ACT Science section. They'll help you refer to the correct visual in a passage, saving you time and confusion. It's a very common mistake to look at the wrong visual, so make sure to spend a few extra seconds figuring out the label of each visual in a passage. Each will be labeled as Figure or Table plus a number. So if there are three visuals, they will be labeled Figure/Table 1, Figure/Table 2, and Figure/Table 3. See below:

In a chemical reaction, the rate expresses the time for the products of the reaction to be generated from the reactants. In the following experiments, a student investigates how different factors affect the rate at which potassium permanganate ($KMnO_4$) is reduced to form manganese (II) ions, carbon dioxide and water after reacting with oxalic acid ($H_2C_2O_4$). As $KMnO_4$ undergoes this reaction it changes in color from purple, to an orange-brown color, and eventually becomes colorless when the reaction is complete.

Experiment 1

A student mixed 15 mL of 1.0 M (moles/liter) $H_2C_2O_4$ in solution with 30 mL sulphuric acid and 60 mL water in a 250 mL beaker. In a separate 100 mL beaker, 15 mL of 0.1 M $KMnO_4$ solution was added. Prior to undergoing any reaction, $KMnO_4$ in solution is purple in color. The two beakers were cooled down to 0°C in an ice bath. The solution of $KMnO_4$ was then added to the second beaker of $H_2C_2O_4$ and sulphuric acid. The time that it took the combined solutions to change color from purple to colorless was recorded. The same protocol was repeated at room temperature (25°) and after warming up both solutions in a water bath of 40°C and 50°C. The results are represented in Table 1.

Table 1

Trial	Temperature (°C)	Reaction Time (sec)
1	0	900
2	25	150
3	40	60
4	50	30

Experiment 2

The same protocol in Experiment 1 was repeated identically, except for that this time a single crystal of manganese sulphate ($KMnO_4$) was added to the solution of $KMnO_4$ prior to mixing with the solution of $H_2C_2O_4$ and sulphuric acid. In this reaction $MnSO_4$ serves as a catalyst. A catalyst is a compound that increases the rate of a reaction but is not consumed in the process. The results from Experiment 2 are shown in Table 2.

Table 2

Trial	Temperature (°C)	Reaction Time (sec)
5	0	282
6	25	52
7	40	28
8	50	14

Experiment 3

Once again the procedure followed in Experiment 1 was repeated, but this time all reactions occurred at room temperature (25°C). In each trial, the concentration of the $H_2C_2O_4$ used varied. The results from Experiment 3 are shown in Table 3.

Table 3

Trial	Concentration of $H_2C_2O_4$ (M)	Reaction Time (sec)
9	0.10	755
10	0.25	541
11	0.50	332
12	0.75	229

Questions on ACT Science will often specifically tell you which figure or table to look at.

In Table 2, what was the slowest reaction time recorded?

A: 755 seconds

B: 900 seconds

C: 282 seconds

D: 541 seconds

The correct answer is C, 282 seconds, which is easy to solve if you remember to look only at Table 2, but if you're skimming the question, you might miss that part and look at all the tables, leading you to choose B, 900 seconds, which is incorrect.

Your first step to answering most ACT Science questions is to make sure you're looking at the correct figure or table referenced in the question. If you're looking at the wrong one to get the answer, you'll almost always get the question wrong.

Axes

Axes are the lines at the side(s) and bottom of a graph. They're needed to figure out the control and the variables in the experiment.

Graphs have an x-axis and y-axis. The x-axis is the horizontal line (typically at the bottom of the graph). The y-axis is the vertical line (typically on the left side of the graph, though more challenging graphs on the ACT Science will have one on the left and one on the right). Let's take a look at this simple graph for practice:

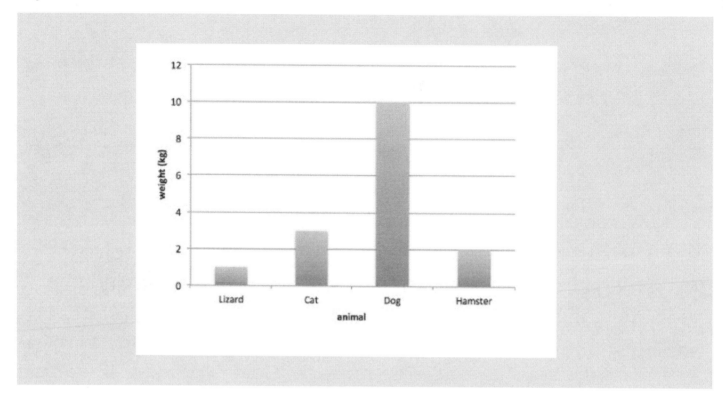

In this graph, the x-axis doesn't measure anything (it only lists animals), while the y-axis measures the animals' weights.

Say the passage had asked: what is the weight of a dog?

First, we need to find "dog" on the axis that defines the type of animal, which is the x-axis. Next, we look on the y-axis for the value of the dog's weight and see that it reads 10 kg.

Now, for practice, let's take a look at a slightly more complicated bar graph with measurements on both axes:

Transient luminous events (TLEs) are short-lived bursts of light that appear in the atmosphere above thunderstorm clouds. TLEs are caused by positive cloud-to-ground (+CG) lightning strokes. However, not every +CG lightning stroke results in a TLE. Figure 1 shows 3 distinct types of TLEs-- elves, red sprites, and blue jets--along with their typical shape, width, and altitude. Table 1 shows the usual duration (in milliseconds, msec) and brightness (in kiloRayleighs, kR) of each type of TLE. Figure 2 contains two graphs: the first shows the number of +CG lightning strokes within ranges of peak electrical currents (in kiloamperes, kA), and the second shows the percentage of those +CG lightning strokes that produced a TLE.

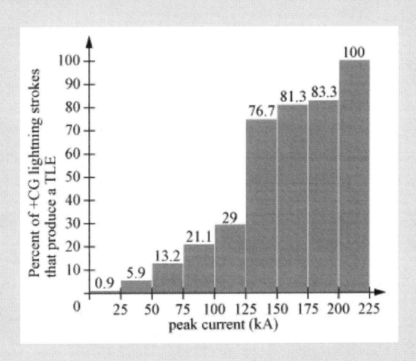

In this graph, the x-axis measures the peak current in kA (kiloamperes), and the y-axis measures the percent of positive cloud-to-ground (+CG) lightning strikes that produce a TLE (transient luminous events, or short-lived bursts of light).

That's a lot of vocab you probably aren't familiar with, but don't let that trick you into thinking the graph is more complicated than it actually is. You don't need to know what kiloamperes, cloud-to-ground lightning strikes, or TLEs are to answer questions about this graph. You just need to be able to understand the (pretty simple) data the graph contains.

For example, what is the percentage of +CG lightning strikes that produce a TLE when the peak current is 150 kA? Again, don't get confused by all the vocab; just find 150 on the x-axis, and look across to see which value it corresponds to on the y-axis. In this case, the test makers have nicely included the y-axis numbers on the bars in the graph, so you can just read the number on top of the bar. So, at 150 kA, about 76.7% of +CG lightning strikes produce a TLE. It's as easy as that.

Scales

Graphs on the ACT Science section include units of measure for each axis next to the label. Don't waste time trying to understand what the units mean. As in the above example, the science section throws in crazy units that you won't have seen unless you studied very high-level physics or chemistry. You don't need to know exactly what they refer to in order to answer the questions.

For ACT Science, the units listed in the answer choices will always match up to the units shown in one of the visuals or mentioned in the passage (such as in the example above). You will not need to convert units from one form of measurement to another (such as converting kiloamperes to amperes). You probably had to do this often in your math or science classes, but ACT Science won't test you on unit conversions.

Types of Charts and Diagrams

Now that you know the basic parts of charts and diagrams, let's look at the visuals that use them. There are four main types of visuals that accompany ACT Science passages. You should be able to recognize and understand each of them.

Bar Graph

Bar graphs tend to be one of the easier visuals you'll see on ACT Science because there will only be one variable shown. This means there's less to understand, so you can interpret these graphs quickly.

Here's a bar graph from the same passage we looked at in the Labels section.

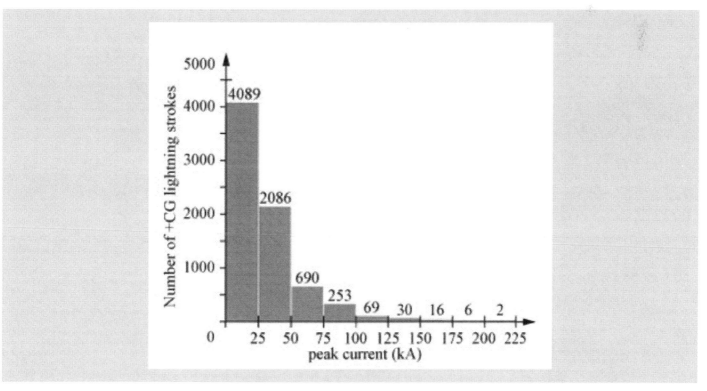

The x-axis is peak current in kA, and the y-axis is number of +CG lightning strikes. (Remember, you don't need to know what kA or +CG lightning strikes are.) Try the following question:

How many +CG lightning strike were there at 115 kA?

A: 253

B: 30

C: 69

D: 690

First, you'd estimate where 115 kA would be on the x-axis, then look on the y-axis for the corresponding value of number of +CG lightning strikes. From looking at the graph, between 100 kA and 125 kA it looks like there are 69 lightning strikes, so the answer would be C.

Bar graphs are pretty simple. Just make sure you've identified the correct bar, and you'll find the data you need.

Scatter Plot

Scatterplots are graphs of plotted points that show the relationship between two sets of data. Here's an example:

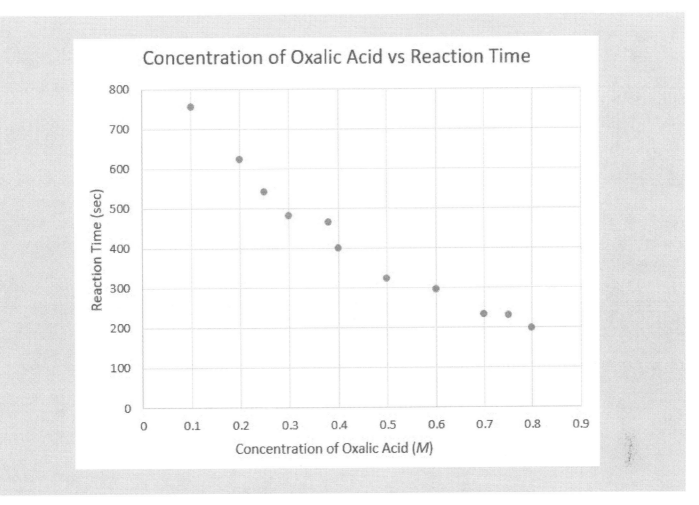

Concentration of Oxalic Acid vs Reaction Time

This scatterplot shows the relationship between the concentration of oxalic acid and reaction time. This means each point represents the reaction time at a certain concentration of oxalic acid.

If a question asked: What was the reaction time at a concentration of 0.5M? You'd find 0.5 on the x-axis, then look on the y-axis for the reaction time of that point. From the graph we can see it's about 320 seconds, so you'd choose whichever answer was closest to that.

Scatterplots can be slightly more challenging if they ask you a question about a point not marked. Let's say you see this question on ACT Science instead:

What is the concentration of oxalic acid when the reaction time is 350 seconds?

A: 0.45M

B: 0.6M

C: 0.35M

D: 0.2M

There is no data point at 350 seconds, and in these cases, we recommend sketching a line that follows the shape of the scatterplot so you can estimate values that don't have specific points.

Here's what that would look like for this example:

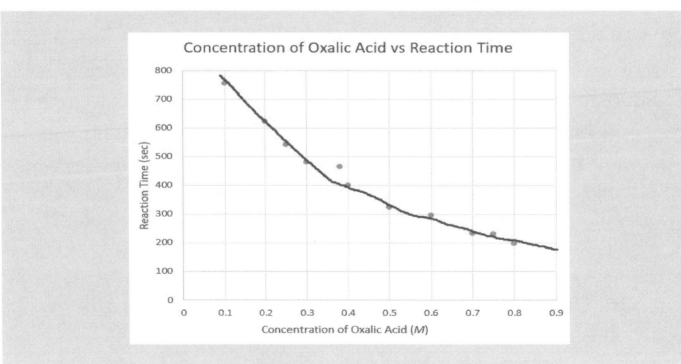

Don't waste time trying to draw a perfect, beautiful line; you just need one that's fairly accurate so you can make estimates from it. Now that we have the line, we can see roughly where 350 seconds would be on it, and follow that to the x-axis. It's between 0.4M and 0.5M, so the correct answer would be A: 0.45M.

Line Graphs

Line graphs are one of the harder types of visuals used in the ACT Science section. The reason they are more difficult is that they show essentially an infinite number of data points, and you need to be precise about which data point you're looking at since each point on the line is a new value.

Below is a line graph similar to those you may see on ACT Science.

The viscosity (resistance to flow) of an ice cream mixture can be determined by measuring the electrical current drawn by the motor rotating the stirring paddle. Figure 3 shows the change in current over a period of mixing time for M1 and 2 other ice cream mixtures (M2 and M3).

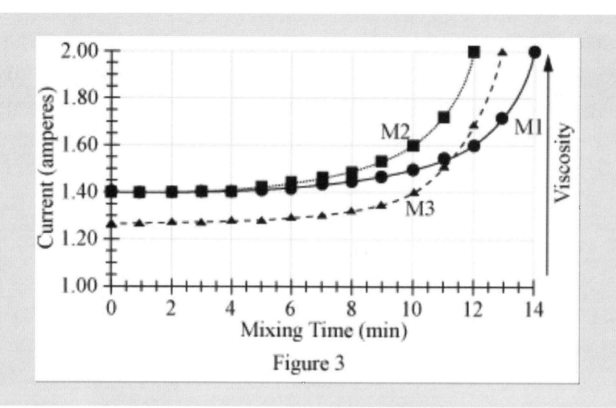

Figure 3

This graph may seem confusing at first glance, so let's break down the information it's showing. By reading the explanation above the graph, we can see that the three lines on the graph (M1, M2, and M3) each represent a different ice cream mixture. Easy enough! The x-axis is the mixing time in minutes, and the y-axis is the current in amperes. The right side of the graph also shows viscosity on the y-axis, and the passage states that viscosity of the ice cream is related to its electrical current.

Like we mentioned before, don't be tempted to try to completely understand the experiment. Electricity in ice cream?! You don't need to get how that works to answer the questions. Just know that each line on the graph represents a different ice cream mixture, each point on the graph shows the current of the ice cream after its been mixed for a certain number of minutes, and viscosity increases with current.

Try this question:

According to this figure, the current drawn after 6 minutes of mixing for M3 is closest to

A: 1.20 amperes

B: 1.30 amperes

C: 1.35 amperes

D: 1.40 amperes

To solve it, first we'd identify M3, which is the line with the triangles. Then we'd find the point on the line that corresponds to 6 minutes on the x-axis. Finally, we'd see where the point we identified hits the y-axis. It can often help to draw a line to the y-axis to see the point of intersection, like this:

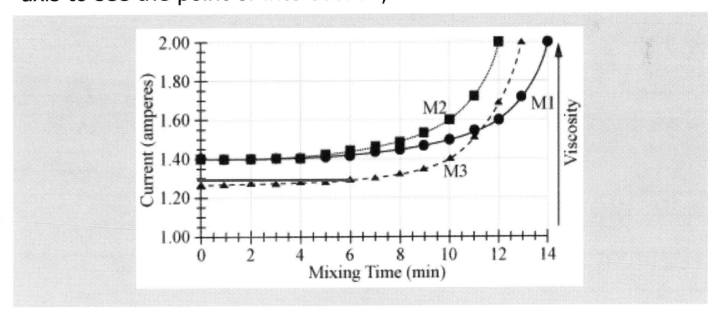

That look to be pretty evenly between 1.2 and 1.4 amperes, so the correct answer is B: 1.30 amperes.

Here's another question:

According to the figure, the current drawn by the motor for M2 was nearer the current drawn for M1 than the current drawn for M3

A: At no times

B: At all times

C: At 11 and 12 minutes

D: From 0 to 10 minutes

For this question, we need to see when M1 was closer to M2 than M3 was. Looking at the graph, M1 and M2 were basically on top of each other from 0-4 minutes. This rules out A and C as answers. At 4 minutes, M1 and M2 begin to gradually move apart, but M1 is still closer to M2 than M3 is. This continues until about 11 minutes, when M1 and M3 intersect. At this point, M1 and M3 are equidistant from M2, and from 11 minutes onward, M3 is closer to M2 than M1 is. Since M1 was closer to M2 than M3 was from 0 to about 10 minutes, that means D is the correct answer.

Tables

Tables are one of the easier types of visuals you'll see on ACT Science. They contain a number of rows and columns, and each individual rectangle is called a cell. Take a look at this example:

Table 2

Particle Category	Weight (g) of Particles				
	Soil 1	Soil 2	Soil 3	Soil 4	Soil 5
Gravel	0	0	0	0	36
Very Coarse Sand	0	132	0	0	54
Coarse Sand	0	241	0	0	197
Medium Sand	0	127	35	134	76
Fine Sand	14	0	136	245	36
Very Fine Sand	11	0	79	96	33

Based on Table 2, the sample with the largest amount, by weight, of fine sand and very fine sand, was:

A: Soil 1

B: Soil 2

C: Soil 4

D: Soil 5

To solve this problem, you'd need to look at the Fine Sand and Very Fine Sand rows. Don't try to add up all those numbers, though; a quick glance will make it obvious that Soil 4 contains the most fine sand and very fine sand (245g and 96g). The correct answer is C: Soil 4.

Some tables on the ACT Science section will have many rows and columns of data and look more confusing, but the technique for finding the correct cell(s) is always the same.

Tricky Graphs

Now you're ready for some more challenging graphs. Here's one that, at first glance, may seem too complicated to understand.

Transient luminous events (TLEs) are short-lived bursts of light that appear in the atmosphere above thunderstorm clouds. TLEs are caused by positive cloud-to-ground (+CG) lightning strokes. However, not every +CG lightning stroke results in a TLE. Figure 1 shows 3 distinct types of TLEs-- elves, red sprites, and blue jets--along with their typical shape, width, and altitude. Table 1 shows the usual duration (in milliseconds, msec) and brightness (in kiloRayleighs, kR) of each type of TLE. Figure 2 contains two graphs: the first shows the number of +CG lightning strokes within ranges of peak electrical currents (in kiloamperes, kA), and the second shows the percentage of those +CG lightning strokes that produced a TLE.

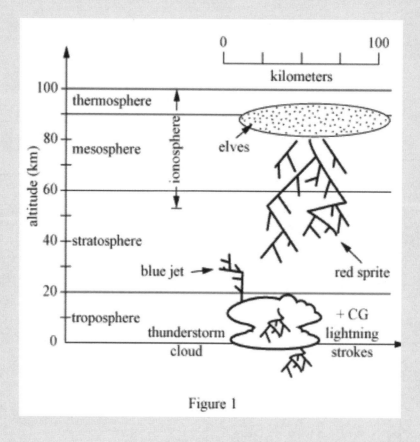

Figure 1

Lightning bolts drawn in the graph? Different levels of the atmosphere? Elves?! How do you even start with this graph?

First, remember that you don't need to understand everything going on in the graph. Also remember that the ACT will often deliberately make graphs look more complicated than they actually are in order to try to confuse you. This is the case here. Once you understand what's going on, the graph is actually pretty simple.

Start by reading the explanation above the graph. "Figure 1 shows 3 distinct types of TLEs- elves, red sprites, and blue jets- along with their typical shape, width, and altitude." Basically, the graph is showing three TLES, what they look like, and where they occur in the atmosphere. Instead of using standard points to depict these TLEs, the test creators decided to draw little pictures of them. This is unusual, which is why it's confusing at first.

Now look for the basics, like axes, labels, and scale. The x-axis is a bit confusing because its label is actually placed above the graph, where the km scale is shown. The y-axis is altitude (again measured in km), and the test makers have taken the additional step of labelling the different parts of the atmosphere. So the axes show the size and altitude of the TLEs.

In addition to the parts of the atmosphere, each of the TLEs is labelled, as well as thunderstorm clouds and +CG lightning strikes. Don't waste time trying to understand what TLEs are, just know there are three of them: elves, red sprites, and blue jets.

This should all be information you process in a minute or two.

Now let's try some questions.

Figure 1 defines which of the following TLES as events that occur in whole or in part in the ionosphere?
  I. Blue jets
  II. Red sprites
  III. Elves

A: I only

B: III only

C: I and II only

D: II and III only

To solve this problem, we need to see which TLEs occur in the ionosphere, so find the ionosphere on the graph. It includes the thermosphere, mesosphere, and the top bit of the stratosphere. The question says only part of the TLE needs to be in the ionosphere, so any TLE with even a little bit in the ionosphere counts. From the graph, elves occur on the border of the thermosphere and mesosphere, so they're in the ionosphere. Red sprites occur in the mesosphere and part of the stratosphere, so they are also in the ionosphere. However, blue jets occur too low to be in the ionosphere. This means the answer is D: II and III only.

Now let's look at question that uses the previous graph as well as this table:

Table 1		
Type of TLE	Duration (msec)	Average Brightness (kR)
Red Sprite	10-100	10
Blue Jet	100-300	800
Elves	<1	1000

A flash was observed above a large thunderstorm cloud. The flash had an average brightness larger than 100 kR and an altitude between 20 and 45 km. Based on Figure 1 and Table 1, the flash was most likely which of the following?

A: Elves

B: A red sprite

C: A blue jet

D: A +CG lightning strike

First the problem states that the average brightness of the flash was more than 100 kR. Looking at Table 1, we can rule out red sprites and +CG lightning strikes based on that. We also know the flash had an altitude between 20 and 45 km. Looking at the graph, elves are found much higher than that altitude, but blue jets occur within that range, so the answer is C: A blue jet.

Recap: Key Tips for Reading Graphs and Charts

Whenever you look at a graph or chart on ACT Science, regardless of how easy or complicated it appears at first glance, follow the below tips to stay focused, weed out extraneous information, and concentrate on the data needed to solve the problems.

- Always read the information that explains what the figures and charts are showing. It often includes key background information that'll make solving questions much easier.

- Read labels very carefully, and make sure you're looking at the correct figure. Once you know you're looking at the right figure, make sure you're also looking at the correct cell, axis, or data point the question is asking about.

- Remember to find the basics - what the axes represent, how the data points are depicted, and what the main purpose of each graph or table is.

- Don't be intimidated by a graph that looks confusing at first glance. Just figure out the basics of what it's showing, then work through the questions one by one, focusing only on the information they ask for. Almost all tables and graphs on ACT Science will contain much more information that you need to know to answer the questions.

- Don't try to understand the units of measure. Don't know what a kiloampere is? That's fine; you don't need to know what it is to answer questions where it's the unit being used.

- Be extra careful when you see a NOT or EXCEPT. These questions are designed to be especially tricky, so read them and the answer choices carefully.

Chapter 5: Understanding Experimental Design

Experimental design refers to how studies/experiments (the ACT tends to use these two words interchangeably) are created and carried out. It includes all the choices scientists make when running the experiments, such as the variable(s) they decide to change, how they measure and record data, and the results they're observing.

Experiments are a major part of ACT Science, and you'll need to be able to understand the types of experiments you'll see in science passages before you can even begin answering questions about them. In this chapter, we explain the different types of studies you'll see in ACT Science, how to analyze them, and how to quickly find the important information in them.

The Two Types of Studies: Observational vs Experimental

There are two main types of studies you'll see in ACT Science: observational and experimental.

In observational studies, scientists simply collect data and study differences. An example would be a study where scientists collected tadpoles from different frog species and recorded their length and weight. The scientists aren't changing or manipulating anything; they're just observing what is already occurring.

In experimental studies, scientists run an experiment where they choose to change certain variables and then see how those changes affect the result. An example would be a study where scientists give tadpoles varying amounts of a certain chemical and observe how it affects their transformation into frogs. In this study, the scientists are actively causing a change since the tadpoles wouldn't otherwise be exposed to the chemical.

In both observational and experimental studies, scientists are looking for the differences between different conditions. It's not that meaningful to just provide a single data point - for example, "green frog tadpoles had an average length of 24 mm." Great, but what does this mean? Is 24 mm large or small? Without comparisons, it's hard to know the importance or meaning of a study.

Therefore, scientists will take multiple data points in different scenarios and then compare them. An ACT Science passage on tadpole size could state that "green frog tadpoles had an average length of 24 mm while spring peeper tadpoles had an average length of 15 mm." Now we can compare the two. Green frog tadpoles had a larger average length than spring peeper tadpoles.

It's also very common for ACT Science to mention multiple studies within a single passage. These studies will be in the same general field, but they will have been conducted by different scientists and may study different aspects of a topic or conduct their studies in different ways. These different studies will be labeled Experiment 1 / 2 / 3 or Study 1 / 2 / 3.

You won't be asked about whether a study is observational or experimental, but being able to correctly place different studies into these two groups will help you figure out the big picture of the study more quickly: were the scientists recording information on what was already happening, or were they trying to change things? Why did they make those decisions? Being able to answer those questions will help you understand the experiment and the scientists' mindset better.

Understanding Observational and Experimental Studies

In the next two sections we look more in-depth at observational and experimental studies. For each type we give an example. Read through it, thinking about key information in the study, then read our analysis and answer the sample question that follows.

When reading a study, remember to skim the passage the way we explained in Chapter 3 so you still have enough time to answer the questions that follow the passage. As you skim, ask yourself the following questions:

- What is the point of this experiment? What is being measured?
- What changes, if any, did the scientists make?
- For passages with multiple studies/experiments: How is each one different from the others?

Observational Studies

Below is an example of a passage on an observational study. Look through it, skimming for important information, then compare what you found to our analysis. Your goal should be to be able to read through shorter passages like this one in about two minutes so you have plenty of time to answer questions.

Soils are composed of mixtures of differently sized particles. Soils can be classified by texture (the composition of the soil based on proportions of sand, silt, and clay particles) and porosity (percent of a soil's total volume composed of open space). Table 1 shows soil particle types with their typical diameters. A well sorted soil is composed of particles with low variation in diameter, while a poorly sorted soil is composed of particles with wide variation in diameter.

Table 1	
Particle Category	Particle Diameter (mm)
Gravel	> 2.0
Very Coarse Sand	1.1-2.0
Coarse Sand	0.6-1.0
Medium Sand	0.26-0.5
Fine Sand	0.14-0.25
Very Fine Sand	0.07-0.13
Silt	0.004-0.06
Clay	< 0.004

Study 1

A 500g sample a soil (Soil 1) was washed through a screen with 0.06mm holes to remove all clay and silt particles. The soil remaining on the screen was dried and weighed, then sifted through a series of screens with progressively smaller holes to separate particles of different categories. The particles collected for each category were then weighed. This procedure was repeated for samples of 4 other soils (Soils 2-5). Table 2 shows the results of this study.

Table 2					
	Weight (g) of Particles				
Particle Category	Soil 1	Soil 2	Soil 3	Soil 4	Soil 5
Gravel	0	0	0	0	36
Very Coarse Sand	0	132	0	0	54
Coarse Sand	0	241	0	0	197
Medium Sand	0	127	35	134	76
Fine Sand	14	0	136	245	36
Very Fine Sand	11	0	79	96	33

Study 2

A sample was taken from each of Soils 1-5 and dried by heating at 101°C for 24 hours, and was then weighed. Table 3 shows the calculated porosity and the void ratio (ratio of the volume of open space to the volume of solid material) of each soil sample.

Table 3		
Soil	Porosity (%)	Void Ratio
1	45	0.82
2	34	0.52
3	43	0.75
4	42	0.72
5	10	0.11

This is an observational study because, even though the scientists sifted and weighed the soil samples, they didn't make any changes to how the soils were composed. Sifting and weighing the samples were just the steps they took to get the data they needed, but no changes were made to the soil samples themselves.

Here's the key information you should have gotten by skimming this passage:

- Point of the study: To learn how different soils are composed, including the particles they contain, porosity, and void ratios
- What changes did the scientists make?: None because this is an observational study

- How did the studies differ from each other? Study 1 analyzed the amount of different particles in the samples, and Study 2 analyzed the porosity and void ratio of the samples.

Experimental Studies

To survive in a medium (a nutrient system) that lacks arginine (an amino acid), E. coli bacteria must synthesize arginine from the medium. A portion of the reaction pathway to synthesize arginine is shown in Figure 1. Each of these reactions is catalyzed by an enzyme (E1-E4). In the first reaction, E1 catalyzes the conversion of the precursor acetylornithine into the product ornithine. In the second reaction, E2 catalyzes the conversion of the precursor ornithine into the product citrulline.

$$\text{acetylornithine} \xrightarrow{E1} \text{ornithine} \xrightarrow{E2} \text{citrulline} \xrightarrow{E3} \text{argininosuccinate} \xrightarrow{E4} \text{arginine}$$

Figure 1

Table 1 shows the E. coli genes that code for the enzymes E1-E4.

Table 1	
Gene	Enzyme
arg 1	E1
arg 2	E2
arg 3	E3
arg 4	E4

A gene can be damaged such that it no longer correctly produces its corresponding enzyme. The pathway then stops at the reaction catalyzed by that enzyme. Consequently, the precursor accumulates and the product is not produced. In standard nomenclature, an undamaged gene is labeled with a plus sign (for example, arg^{1+}). A damaged gene that cannot produce its enzyme is labeled with a minus sign (for example, arg^{1-}).

Experiment

A biologist grew wild-type (naturally occurring) E. coli on minimal medium (MM), a medium that does not contain arginine.

The biologist then irradiated the E. coli to cause genetic damage. Next, she identified E. coli that could no longer synthesize arginine in MM. She created five variations of media and tested these E. coli on each media to observe growth. Table 2 shows classification of E. coli into 5 types depending on the media on which they grew. An "x" indicates that a given type could grow on the corresponding medium and therefore could synthesize arginine from that medium.

Table 2					
	Type				
Medium	1	2	3	4	5
MM					
MM+acetylornithine					x
MM+ornithine	x				x
MM+citrulline	x	x			x
MM+argininosuccinate	x	x	x		x

- Point of the study: To learn which media damaged E. coli could synthesize arginine on.
- What changes did the scientists make?: Damaged E. coli so it couldn't synthesize arginine on some media.
- How did the studies differ from each other? There was only one experiment in this passage.

Recap: What You Need to Know About Experimental Design

When reading about experiments in ACT Science, you need to be able to find key information quickly. Both skimming so quickly that you miss the point of the experiment and reading so carefully that you run out of time when answering questions will hurt your science score.

Practice is the best way to develop this skill and get faster at it. Every time you read a passage, concentrate on skimming the passage and finding key information quickly. When reading about an experiment in ACT Science, remember to ask yourself the following questions:

- What is the point of this experiment? What is being measured?
- What changes, if any, did the scientists make?
- For multiple studies/experiments: How is each one different from the others?

Once you learn how to efficiently identify the main facts of an experiment, you'll have an easier time answering questions because you'll understand what was going on in the experiment, and you won't need to keep jumping back up to the passage to find key information again.

Chapter 6: The Science You Need to Know

As we mentioned previously, you don't need to know scientific facts to answer the vast majority of questions on ACT Science. However, for roughly three questions out of the 40, you'll need to have some basic scientific background knowledge in order to solve the problem.

There's no need to start rereading your freshman science textbook though; in this section we go over every one of the thirteen science subjects you're expected to know for ACT Science. For each topic, we'll explain exactly what information you need to know about it so you're not spending studying material you won't see on the exam. These are the topics the ACT expects you to know and by reviewing them, especially if your science class grades in school weren't stellar, you'll ensure you have all the scientific background knowledge you need for the ACT.

Reminder: ACT Science Tests Understanding, Not Knowledge

As we mentioned earlier in the book, ACT Science is not designed to test your knowledge of scientific facts. They even state outright that "Advanced knowledge in these subjects is not required, but background knowledge acquired in general, introductory science courses is needed to answer some of the questions. The test emphasizes scientific reasoning skills over recall of scientific content, skill in mathematics, or reading ability." For the majority of ACT Science questions, you'll be given all the background information you need to answer the question, and important terms will be explained in the passages.

So, you don't need to be a biology whiz or a chemistry genius to do well on ACT Science.
However, the ACT does say that "background knowledge" will be required, and for some questions on the science section, you will need to have some basic scientific knowledge in order to find the correct answer. In this chapter we go over the thirteen science topics the ACT expects you to know on exam day.

Topic 1: Cell Biology

For cell biology, you need to know the names of key cell organelles (parts of cells), their function, and whether they are found in animal cells, plant cells, or both. All of the organelles below are found in both plant and animal cells, except for chloroplasts, which are only found in plant cells.

Lysosomes contain enzymes that are used to digest food for the cell (similar to how the stomach digests food for the body) or break down the cell when it dies.

Mitochondria are organelles that act like a digestive system. They take in nutrients (fats, sugars and proteins), break the nutrients down, and create energy-rich molecules (ATP) for the cell. They are often known as the "powerhouse" of the cell because of all the energy they produce.

The **cell nucleus** acts as the brain of the cell. It contains the cell's DNA, or the genetic information, which makes proteins (see Topic 2). The nucleus also helps control major processes in the cell, such as eating and reproduction.

Ribosomes build proteins by connecting amino acids into long chains.

Chloroplasts only exist in plant cells. They assist in the process of photosynthesis, converting light into energy (which only plants do, not animals).

The **cell membrane** holds all of the organelles of the cell and serves as the barrier between the cell and other cells.

Here's a sample question:

Students studying cells under a microscope are trying to determine whether the cells they are looking at belong to an animal or a plant. Viewing which organelle in the cells would help them come to a definitive conclusion?

A: Lysosomes

B: Cell membrane

C: Chloroplasts

D: Golgi Apparatus

If you studied the information above, you'll know that the answer is C, chloroplasts, since these only exist in plant cells. All the other organelles are found in both plant and animal cells.

Topic 2: DNA, RNA, Ribosomes, and Protein Synthesis

DNA contains the genetic information needed to make proteins. Protein synthesis requires DNA, RNA, ribosomes, and proteins. The DNA acts as the blueprint for protein production.

Messenger RNA (known as mRNA) makes a copy of the DNA code of a specific gene. This process is known as transcription, and it occurs in the nucleus.

Once the mRNA is made, it leaves the nucleus and enters the cytosol (fluid) of the cell. Ribosomes use mRNA as a guide to make proteins. The process of producing protein from the mRNA is known as translation.

As a quick review, protein synthesis consists of two steps: DNA to mRNA (transcription) and mRNA to protein (translation).

Here's a sample question:

Which of the following statements best explains why Study 1 did not yield the results the scientists expected?

A: Transcription only occurs in the nuclei of cells and is done to create DNA

B: Transcription only occurs in the nuclei of cells and is done to create mRNA

C: Transcription only occurs in the cytosol and is done to create DNA

D: Transcription only occurs in the cytosol and is done to create mRNA

The correct answer is B.

Topic 3: Natural Selection

Natural selection is also known as "survival of the fittest." Natural selection states that, in a specific environment, traits that allow organisms to reproduce more effectively will become more common, and traits that reduce reproductive success will become less common. A classic example of this is the change in peppered moth color during the Industrial Revolution.

In England, the burning of coal during the Industrial Revolution changed tree bark from light brown to dark brown in color. When this happened, the dark-colored peppered moths blended in perfectly and were hidden from predators. Their numbers increased. However, the number of light-colored peppered moths drastically decreased because they were now getting eaten much more often. This meant there were fewer of them to reproduce.

Once clean air acts were passed, another change occurred. Trees quickly returned to a lighter color, making the darker moths easily visible to predators. Meanwhile, lighter moths were now hidden from view and survived to lay eggs. Lighter moths became more numerous and darker moths became rarer. Natural selection caused the numbers of light and dark moths to change over the years based on which color was best for survival at the time.

Try this question:

Which of the following scenarios is NOT an example of natural selection?

A: An elk population whose average antler size has decreased after hunters killed the majority of elk with larger antlers.

B: Giraffes with longer necks surviving better than those with shorter necks in an area where low trees and branches were destroyed by widespread fires.

C: Peacocks with brighter colors in their tail feathers having more offspring because they're more attractive to female peahens.

D: Bird species that able to build nests atop buildings surviving better than birds who can only build their nests in trees in an area where a forest was razed to make room for a new shopping center.

The correct answer is A, since it is the only option where the change was due directly to humans. The elk with smaller antlers don't have better survival skills or adaptations; they're just less attractive to hunters so they happen to be killed less.

You might have been unsure if D was the correct answer since humans removed the forest and create the shopping center was caused by humans. However, like the example with the moths, humans only created the catalyst for the change, namely the pollution and shopping center, not the change itself. This is different than choice A where humans were directly altering a population by killing elk with certain traits.

Topic 4: Basic Molecule Structure

The science section expects you to know the basic molecular structure of sugars, fats, proteins, and nucleic acids.

$C_6H_{12}O_6$ is the molecular formula of the sugar glucose. This formula commonly shows up on the ACT, so be sure you can recognize it.

There are many different kinds of fats, including saturated, unsaturated, and trans fats. The test does not expect you to know each structure. You only need to know that fats are made up of C (carbon), H (hydrogen), and O (oxygen) molecules and be able to differentiate fats from sugars. Fats have nearly twice the number of H molecules as C molecules, and fats also have a very small number of O molecules compared to sugars. Fats are also much larger in size than sugar. For example, an unsaturated fat triglyceride has a chemical formula of $C_{55}H_{98}O_6$.

Proteins are composed of amino acids. There are many different protein structures, but all proteins contain C, H, O and N (nitrogen) molecules.

Nucleic acids are biomolecules. Two types of nucleic acids that we already discussed are DNA and RNA. Nucleic acids are made up of three parts: a 5-carbon sugar, a phosphate group, and a nitrogenous base. Nucleic acids are different from sugars, fats, and proteins because they are made up of P (phosphorus) in addition to C, H, N, and O.

Topic 5: Freezing/Boiling Point of Water in Celsius

Water freezes at 0 degrees Celsius and boils at 100 degrees Celsius. That is all you need to know for this topic. Memorize those numbers.

Topic 6: pH Scale

The pH scale is a measure of how acidic or basic a substance is. All you need to know is that a pH of below 7 is acidic, above 7 is basic, and at 7 is considered neutral. For some examples, Coca Cola has a pH of 2.5 (very acidic), water typically has a pH of 7 (neutral), and baking soda has a pH of 9 (basic).

Topic 7: Molar Mass Concepts

The only molar mass concept you need to know is that the mass of a molecule equals the sum of the mass of its atoms. For example, if there's an ACT question asking about oxygen's weight versus carbon dioxide's weight, you would need to know that O_2 is lighter per molecule than CO_2 because CO_2 has an extra carbon atom that oxygen doesn't have.

Topic 8: How Charges Interact

Atoms are composed of three types of particles: protons, electrons, and neutrons. Protons are positively charged, electrons are negatively charged, and neutrons have no charge.

Like charges repel each other while opposite charges attract each other. For example, two positive charges will repel each other while a positive and a negative charge will attract.

Topic 9: Phase Changes

We already mentioned the freezing and boiling point of water in Celsius, but you also need to know the order of phase changes. Below freezing point a material will be in solid form, just above freezing point a material will be in liquid form, and above boiling point a liquid becomes a gas (is vaporized).

One natural way to think about this is in terms of water. When it's really cold, water turns to ice (solid). When it warms up, water turns to liquid. Then, when you boil it, water turns to steam (gas).

Here's a sample question:

In a controlled experiment, if the temperature changes from 78 degrees Celsius to 112 degrees Celsius, what will happen to a sample of water that is being studied?

A: It will freeze

B: It will remain in the same state

C: It will condense

D: It will vaporize

Topic 10: Gravity

You'll need to know that gravity is a downward force that acts on objects, and other forces (such as a spring or pulley) can counteract gravity. This will come up frequently in passages that show experiments using springs or pulleys.

Topic 11: Density Formula

Density is the degree of compactness of a substance. To calculate the density of a substance, you use the formula:

Density = mass/volume

So, if an object has a mass of 455 grams and a volume of 230 cm³, then its density is 455 g/ 230 cm³ or 1.98 g/ cm³

Try this sample question:

Student 1 is analyzing the properties of an unknown liquid. He knows its mass is 200 g and its density is 1.5 g/mL. The volume of the liquid is closest to:

A: 150 mL

B: 110 mL

C: 142 mL

D: 133 mL

This problem is a little bit different because it's a liquid instead of a solid and you're being given density and mass and told to find volume. However, you're still using the same equation.

Density = mass/volume

1.5 = 200 / V   First multiply both sides by V

1.5 (V) = 200   Now divide both sides by

V = 200 / 1.5

You'll need to do some long division to work out 200/1.5, and you may find it easier to move the decimal place to the right one spot for each number so you're calculating 2000/15. You'll get 133.33333 which is closest to answer choice D. Also remember that you don't need to worry about units on ACT Science, so you can ignore the units when doing calculations to make things simpler.

Topic 12: Density Rules

In addition to the formula for density, you also need to know the main density rule: denser objects sink, and less dense objects float. Objects only float when they are less dense than the liquid they are placed in.

An easy way to think about this: what happens when you throw a rock into water? It sinks. That's because the rock is denser than water, meaning it weighs more at the same volume.

What about when you throw a styrofoam cup into water? It floats —because styrofoam is less dense than water. At the same volume, styrofoam weighs less than water. Water has a density of 1 g/cm^3, so anything with a density less than that will float in water, and anything with a density greater than that will sink in water.

Topic 13: Basic Math Skills

You will also need to know some math for the ACT Science section, but only very basic skills, so as long as you feel set for ACT Math, you'll be more than prepared for the math on the science section. The math you need to know for ACT Science is typically basic arithmetic and how to make estimates.

Here's an example:

Based on the results of Experiment 2, if the distance from the center of a 50m x 50m plot was 85m from the nearest body of water, the expected soil porosity at the plot would be closest to which of the following values?

A: 45%

B: 49%

C: 43%

D: 41%

Distance to Nearest Body of Water (m)	Soil Porosity (%)
50	31
60	33
70	37
80	41
90	45
100	47

The question wants to know soil porosity for a plot that's 85 m from the nearest body of water, but 85 m isn't included in the table. This means we'll need to do some interpolation. Both 80 m and 90 m are included in the table, and since 85 m is equidistant from those two points, we can simply find the average soil porosity of those two points to estimate the porosity at 85 m.

The calculation for this is: (Sum of the values)/(Number of values)

= (45 + 41)/2
= 86/2
=43

The correct answer is C, 43%. To solve this problem, you only need to do some simple addition and division which is typical of the calculations you'll need to be able to do on ACT Science. The sample problem in Topic 11 is another example of the type of calculations you'll be expected to do for ACT Science.

What If You See an Unfamiliar Concept?

There's always a small chance the ACT decides to break its own rules and ask a question about a science topic that isn't covered here, or you may just forget one of these facts on the day of the exam. What should you do if you see a question on a topic you don't know much or anything about?

First, don't panic. This is just one question on one section of the exam, and even if you miss it, you can still get a high ACT score.

Second, don't waste a lot of time staring at the question and trying to go through everything you may remember on the topic. Remember, you don't want to spend more than 90 seconds on any science question because doing so can hurt your score much more than just one incorrect answer.

Next, look at the answer choices. Are there any choices you definitely know are the wrong answer? This often happens even if you don't know much about the topic the question is asking about. For example, if the question is about fats, you may not remember anything about the different types of fats, but if one of the answers is glucose, you may be able to cross that choice off by remembering that glucose is a sugar, not a fat.

Finally, once you've done the best you can, just pick a option out of the remaining choices and move onto the next question. Don't let one missed question affect your concentration or confidence.

Recap: Key Concepts for ACT Science

Even though you don't need background scientific knowledge to answer most questions on ACT Science, you'll likely have a few questions on exam day that require you to know some scientific facts. Being well versed on the topics in this chapter will give you a great chance of answering them correctly.

Additionally, having a solid grounding of basic scientific facts can help you feel more confident during ACT Science when you see passages on topics you know, even if you don't directly use those facts to answer the questions. For example, if a question gives melting points of different samples and asks if they'll be liquid or solid at a given temperature, you'll likely be able to find the answer from an included graph or chart, but having a background knowledge of melting points can help you answer the question faster and feel more confident in your answer.

Chapter 7: Reading Strategies for ACT Science Passages

You may not think that reading a science passage requires a lot of strategy, but the way you choose to approach an ACT Science passage and its accompanying questions can make or break your score for this section. Many students taking the ACT don't realize that there are many strategies you can use to read ACT Science passages more efficiently.

In this chapter, you'll learn about reading strategies you can use for each of the passage types you'll see in ACT Science. We also include sample passages with our notes on what information you should be paying attention to and what information can be ignored so you can learn how to quickly and accurately read science passages.

Review: The 3 Types of ACT Science Passages

In Chapter 1, we took an in-depth look at the three types of passages you'll see on ACT Science, but here's a quick refresher.

Data Representation passages and Research Summaries passages are very similar. While Data Representation passages typically focus on multiple experiments and Research Summaries passages typically focus on one experiment, both use visuals (graphs, tables, etc.) as the primary way to convey information. We recommend the same three reading approaches for both these passage types.

Conflicting Viewpoints passages differ from the other two passage types in that they typically don't have visuals. For this passage type, we suggest two different reading approaches.

For each ACT Science passage type, we'll describe multiple ways of approaching the passage and questions. No one way is better than another; it's all about what's finding which method works best for you. Different students have different styles of test taking, and having multiple options will make it easier to find the reading strategy that helps you get your highest ACT Science score.

Reading Strategies for Data Representation and Research Summaries Passages

In this section we discuss three methods of approaching Data Representation and Research Summaries passages. Even if you have a reading strategy that you think works pretty well, we recommend trying each of the methods below at least once. You never know if you'll find a method you like better!

Method 1: Skim the Passage, Then Read the Questions

This is the approach we recommend most students start with. It's a good balance between the other two methods, and it works for many students who take the ACT.

Using this method, you'll first quickly skim the passage, looking for the main ideas of the experiment(s) and visuals. Keywords to look for include trends such as "increase" or "decrease" and those that suggest differences, such as "high," "low," "big," or "small." Circle or underline important parts of the passage as you skim. You may also find it helpful to write a few notes in the margin, but keep these brief since taking too many notes will use up a lot of your time. Your goal should be to spend about one to two minutes, at most, skimming the passage.

In Chapter 3 we went over an example of what passage skimming looks like. Here's another passage with our skimming notes included.

Soils are composed of mixtures of differently sized particles. Soils can be classified by texture (the composition of the soil based on proportions of sand, silt, and clay particles) and porosity (percent of a soil's total volume composed of open space). Table 1 shows soil particle types with their typical diameters. A well sorted soil is composed of particles with low variation in diameter, while a poorly sorted soil is composed of particles with wide variation in diameter.

Notes: Soil is made of different particles. Texture = amounts of sand, silt, and clay in a soil. Porosity = percent of open space in a soil.

Table 1	
Particle Category	Particle Diameter (mm)
Gravel	> 2.0
Very Coarse Sand	1.1-2.0
Coarse Sand	0.6-1.0
Medium Sand	0.26-0.5
Fine Sand	0.14-0.25
Very Fine Sand	0.07-0.13
Silt	0.004-0.06
Clay	< 0.004

Notes: This table shows the sizes of different particles. Gravel is biggest; clay is smallest.

Study 1

A 500g sample a soil (Soil 1) was washed through a screen with 0.06mm holes to remove all clay and silt particles. The soil remaining on the screen was dried and weighed, then sifted through a series of screens with progressively smaller holes to separate particles of different categories. The particles collected for each category were then weighed. This procedure was repeated for samples of 4 other soils (Soils 2-5). Table 2 shows the results of this study.

Notes: Five soil samples were sorted and weighed. That's all we need to take from this! The exact way the soils were sorted is not important to know right now.

| | \multicolumn{5}{c}{Table 2} |
| | | | | | |

| | \multicolumn{5}{c}{Weight (g) of Particles} |
Particle Category	Soil 1	Soil 2	Soil 3	Soil 4	Soil 5
Gravel	0	0	0	0	36
Very Coarse Sand	0	132	0	0	54
Coarse Sand	0	241	0	0	197
Medium Sand	0	127	35	134	76
Fine Sand	14	0	136	245	36
Very Fine Sand	11	0	79	96	33

Notes: This table shows the weight of different particles for the five soil samples. (We're not going to worry about the compositions of specific soils right now, so don't waste time reading the data in the table.)

Study 2

A sample was taken from each of Soils 1-5 and dried by heating at 101°C for 24 hours, and was then weighed. Table 3 shows the calculated porosity and the void ratio (ratio of the volume of open space to the volume of solid material) of each soil sample.

Notes: The porosity and void ratios of the five soil samples were measured and recorded. (Again, minor details like what temperature the soils were heated to or how long they were heated are not important to know right now. Skip right over them.)

Table 3		
Soil	Porosity (%)	Void Ratio
1	45	0.82
2	34	0.52
3	43	0.75
4	42	0.72
5	10	0.11

Notes: This table shows the porosity and void ratio of the soil samples. We're not going to worry about looking at the actual data until a question specifically requires it.

Did you notice that, while skimming the passage, we actually ignored most of the information it contained? We were only looking for main ideas: what the point of the experiment was, key steps in the experiment, and the main idea tables/graphs were showing. Smaller details like individual steps in an experiment and what specific cells/points in the visuals were showing were skipped over during skimming. These little details contain so much information, and so little of it is actually asked about in the questions, that we didn't bother spending our time on it during skimming.

Method 2: Skip the Passage and Go Right to the Questions

For this method, you'll skip the passage and go straight to the questions. Try to answer the questions by using only the graphs, charts, and other visuals being referenced. If you need more information to answer a particular question, skip it and come back to it after answering as many questions as you can with the visuals alone. When you return to the questions you skipped, skim the passage for the information needed to answer these remaining questions.

Most students prefer to at least skim the passage before going straight to the questions, but there are actually a fair amount of ACT Science questions you can answer without reading the passage at all. Instead, you can just look at the visual being referenced in the question. Here's an example from the same passage we went over for Method 1.

Table 2					
	Weight (g) of Particles				
Particle Category	Soil 1	Soil 2	Soil 3	Soil 4	Soil 5
Gravel	0	0	0	0	36
Very Coarse Sand	0	132	0	0	54
Coarse Sand	0	241	0	0	197
Medium Sand	0	127	35	134	76
Fine Sand	14	0	136	245	36
Very Fine Sand	11	0	79	96	33

Permeability is a measure of how fast water moves through a soil. It is known that permeability increases as the proportion, by weight, of a soil's particles that are coarse sand size or larger increases. Based on the results of Table 2, which two of the following soils most likely have nearly the same permeability?

A: Soil 1 and Soil 2

B: Soil 2 and Soil 3

C: Soil 3 and Soil 4

D: Soil 4 and Soil 5

This question is asking about permeability, which is helpfully defined right in the question. We're asked to find the two soils with the closest permeability. In the question, it states that permeability is affected by the size of the sand particles. This means that the two soils with the closest permeability will be the soils with the most similar amounts of each particle.

Looking at the table, we can see Soils 3 and 4 are most similar because neither of them contain gravel, very coarse sand, or coarse sand, but they each contain medium sand, fine sand, and very fine sand. The correct answer is C, and we were able to answer that question by skipping the passage entirely and just going straight to the visual the question referenced.

This method may be the best approach for you if you struggle to skim passages quickly enough, have trouble picking the important information out of a passage, and/or frequently run out of time on ACT Science. By skipping the passage, you avoid the need to read it all the way through; instead you only look at the parts you need to read to answer a handful of remaining questions.

However, some students dislike this method because jumping between the passage and the questions throws them off, and they can end up wasting time hunting through the passage for the information they need to answer each question.

Method 3: Read the Whole Passage First

This is the method most students follow before they learn about ACT Science reading strategies. Even though it's popular, we actually don't recommend this method for most students.

Some students think that by reading the entire passage first they won't need to go back to it once they begin answering questions, However, this almost never happens. Many ACT Science questions ask about specific details in a visual or experiment, and it would be almost impossible to remember all of this information while reading the passage for the first time. Additionally, most of the information in the passage is not needed to answer any of the questions, so doing a close read of it will waste time you can't afford to be wasting.

If you plan on using this approach, you need to be able to read the passage/visuals in less than two minutes since you only have five minutes to complete each passage. Set aside at least three minutes to answer questions.

If you're targeting a score between 31 and 36 and aren't able to get your reading pace under two minutes, don't use this strategy, or you won't be able to finish all seven passages. If you are targeting a score of 30 or below, you can afford to skip one passage, so you could use this strategy if your reading pace is slower.

Even if you feel most comfortable using this method, we

recommend trying at least a couple of sample questions using Method 1, the skimming method. With enough practice, you'll become better at quickly reading a passage and pulling out the bits of information that are actually important for the questions.

Reading Approach for the Conflicting Viewpoints Passage

We recommend you approach the Conflicting Viewpoints passages differently than the rest of the passages in ACT Science. Since Conflicting Viewpoints passages often don't have visuals, it would be ineffective to try to skip over the passage completely and go directly to the questions. You'd end up going back to the passage for every question. Instead, we suggest two other reading strategies for this passage type.

Method 1: Read the Whole Passage First

We don't recommend this strategy for most students when reading Research Summaries and Data Representation passages, but this is the best strategy for the Conflicting Viewpoints passage. Nearly every Conflicting Viewpoints question refers to information in the passage, and questions are often about minor differences between the scientists'/students' viewpoints. Reading the entire passage first and then going to the questions is actually faster than jumping back to the passage for every question.

While reading the passage, you should ask yourself these questions:

- What does scientist/student 1 believe?
- What does scientist/student 2 believe?
- What does scientist/student 3/4/5 believe? (Occasionally, there will be more than two viewpoints represented. There have been some passages with up to five different viewpoints.)
- How is scientist/student 2's point of view similar to scientist/student 1's point of view?
- How is scientist/student 2's point of view different from scientist/student 1's point of view?

You'll likely need all this information to answer the Conflicting Viewpoints questions. Since it can be hard to get that information from just skimming the passage, we recommend reading the entire passage as the most effective strategy for Conflicting Viewpoints.

Here's a Conflicting Viewpoints passage with our notes on the key information we read.

In Cycas revoluta (a species of seed plant), males have cones that produce pollen, and females have cones that produce seeds. Pollination requires the movement of pollen from inside a male cone to inside a female cone, where multiple ovules are located and pollinated. The ovules then develop into seeds. Below, two students discuss this pollination process.

Experiments
The students proposed 3 experiments using a Cycas revoluta population in an area with sap beetles and in which the percentage of ovule pollination in normally 99% (see table).

Experiment	Procedure
1	Some female *Cycas revoluta* cones are covered with plastic bags that exclude insects and wind.
2	Some female *Cycas revoluta* cones are covered with mesh bags that exclude insects, but not wind.
3	Some female *Cycas revoluta* cones are covered with cylinders that exclude wind, but not insects.

Student 1

In Cycas revoluta, 80% of ovule pollination results from insect pollination, and 20% results from wind pollination. These are the only two pollination mechanisms.

Cycas revoluta have mutually beneficial relationships with certain species of insects. Sap beetles swarm male Cycas revoluta cones when these cones are releasing pollen. When they enter the cones, the sap beetles become covered with the plant's pollen. The sap beetles then visit the female Cycas revoluta cones and deposit some of the pollen when it rubs off them. In the absence of sap beetles, the percent of ovule pollination in Cycas revoluta is about 20%.

Wind pollination is infrequent because Cycas revoluta pollen is large and heavy, making it difficult for it to travel long distances by wind. Additionally, the openings in the female cones are aligned horizontally, so wind-borne pollen must be blown horizontally in order to enter these cones.

Student 2

Wind pollination causes the majority, about 90%, of Cycas revoluta pollination, while only about 10% of ovule pollination in Cycas revoluta is caused by insects. Without wind pollination, the percent of ovule pollination decreases by 90%. If neither of these processes occur, the percent of ovule pollination decreases by 100%.

Wind tunnel experiments show that the shape of the female Cycas revoluta cones creates air currents that facilitate the horizontal movement of pollen into these cones so it is easier for windborne pollen to enter. Additionally, male Cycas revoluta cones produce enormous quantities of pollen, a trait that is common only in wind-pollinated plants. This means the majority of pollen can miss the female cones and the cones will still be pollinated because so much pollen is carried by the wind.

Pollination by sap beetles is infrequent because the beetles prefer other plant species over Cycas revoluta and only rarely visit Cycas revoluta, minimizing the amount of pollination they can perform.

Key Information From the Passage:
- Student 1 believes majority of pollination is from insects
- Student 2 believes majority of pollination is from wind
- Ways Student 1's and Student 2's beliefs are similar: both believe wind and insect pollination are the only types of pollination for this plant species.
- Ways Student 1's and Student 2's beliefs are different: Student 1 believes the majority of pollination is from insects and that wind pollination is rare because the pollen is heavy and the openings of the female cones make it difficult for windblown pollen to enter.
- Student 2 believes the majority of pollination is from wind and pollination by beetles is rare because sap beetles only rarely visit this species.

You could potentially get all this information by just skimming the passage, but you also run the risk of missing an important piece information that you may need when answering questions.

Here's a sample question:

Based on the experiments described in the table, Students 1 and 2 would most likely agree that the percent of ovule pollination would be highest in female Cycas revoluta cones that are:

A: covered with plastic bags that block wind and insects

B: not covered with a bag or cylinder

C: covered with mesh bags that block insects

D: covered with cylinders that block wind

To answer this question, we need to remember the key information we looked for in the passage, specifically the points Student 1 and Student 2 agreed on and the points they disagreed on. Student 1 believes the majority of Cycas revoluta pollination is from insects while Student 2 believes it's from wind.

This means Student 1 wouldn't agree with answer choice C, and Student 2 wouldn't agree with answer choice D; so they're both out. Answer choice A is incorrect because both students agree wind and insects are the only methods of pollination, and if the cones were covered in plastic bags, there'd be no pollination at all. That leaves answer choice B as the correct answer.

Method 2: Skim the Questions, Then Read the Passage

Another method is skimming the questions first to get a sense of what you should be paying attention to in the passage, then reading the passage, then answering the questions.

This is the preferred method of some students, but it may slow you down too much to finish the section in time since you'll effectively be reading each question twice. We recommend trying Method 1 first, then trying this method if you think it'll work better for you.

Recap: ACT Science Passage-Reading Strategies

Knowing how to approach the passages on ACT Science will make all the difference in how quickly and accurately you're able to answer the questions in this section.

For the Data Representation and Research Summaries passages we recommend skimming the passage first and then going to the questions. This allows you to get a general idea of the information the passage contains without wasting time trying to remember irrelevant details you won't be asked about.

For the Conflicting Viewpoints passage, we recommend reading the entire passage before you begin answering questions since there are no/few visuals for this passage and all the questions will refer to information you can only find by reading the passage.

However, there are different methods you can use for each of the passages. For Data Representation and Research Summaries passages, you could also skip the passage and go straight to the questions or read the entire passage before tackling the questions. For Conflicting Viewpoints, you could also skim the questions before reading the passage so you have a better of what to pay attention to.

Choose the reading strategy for each passage type that works best for you. This will be the strategy that allows you to accurately answer questions in a timely way. The only way to figure out which method is best for you is to get in a lot of practice. While you're answering practice ACT Science questions, try out different methods and see which feels most comfortable and helps you solve questions fastest. That's the reading method you want to use on exam day.

Chapter 8: How to Solve Data Representation Questions

Data Representation questions, which ask primarily about the graphs, tables, and other visuals that accompany a passage, can be challenging even if you feel comfortable analyzing scientific data. The ACT will often purposely make their visuals confusing or overly-complicated so that it's hard to see the correct answer, even when it's right in front of you. In this chapter, we give you tips and strategies for solving Data Representation questions so you can see through the tricks the ACT tries in these questions and find the correct answer.

Types of Data Representation Questions

There are three main types of Data Representation questions: fact finding, interpreting questions, and calculations and estimates. For each of these question types, we'll explain what they'll look like and the information they'll ask you about, and we'll work through sample questions.

Fact-Finding Questions

Fact-finding questions are one of the most straightforward ACT

Science question types: they simply ask you to relay information that's presented in the passage. To answer these questions, you'll need to read and analyze the graphs, tables, and scatterplots accompanying a passage. For the simplest fact-finding questions, you'll only need to find specific data points that are already in the visuals. However, more complicated questions will require more analysis.

Try this sample question:

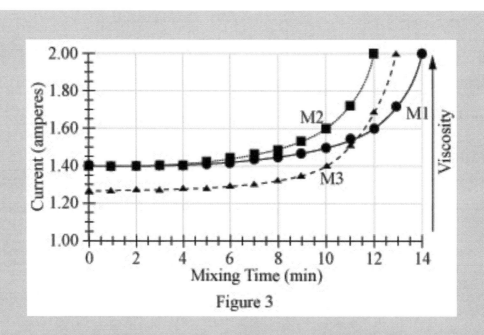

Figure 3

According to Figure 3, the current drawn after 6 minutes of mixing for M3 is closest to

A: 1.20 amperes

B: 1.30 amperes

C: 1.35 amperes

D: 1.40 amperes

This is one of the more straightforward Fact-Finding questions. To solve it, we only need to find where the M3 plot is at six minutes of mixing time. The M3 plot is one with triangles on it. Find where six minutes of mixing time is on the x-axis, find the M3 plot, and look to the left to see where it hits the y-axis. It can sometimes help to draw a line on the graph to help find the point you're looking for, like this:

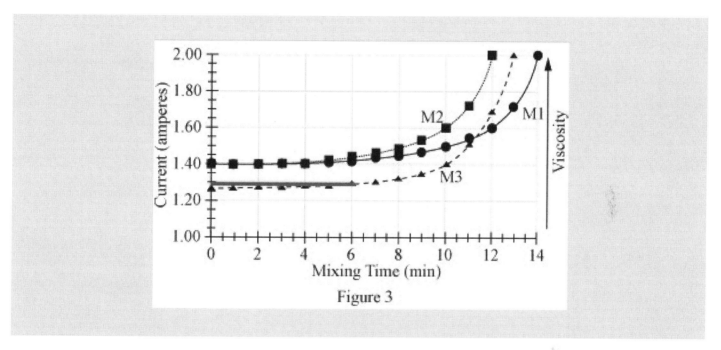

Figure 3

Looking at where the line hits on the y-axis, where can see it's between 1.20 and 1.40 amperes. This means the answer is either B or C. If you look closely at the y-axis, you can see that it's scaled so that each little line on the axis represents an increase of 0.05 amperes. The line we drew hits the y-axis two lines after 1.20 amperes, which means it's at 1.30 amperes, making B the correct answer choice.

This was a pretty simple question to answer, but just make sure you're being careful when you draw lines on the graphs so that you get an accurate estimate. If we'd been slightly off on our drawing, we might have thought the answer was 1.35 amperes instead and marked the wrong answer.

Here's a more challenging Fact-Finding question:

Table 2 shows classification of E. coli into 5 types depending on the media on which they grew. An "x" indicates that a given type could grow on the corresponding medium and therefore could synthesize arginine from that medium.

Table 2					
			Type		
Medium	1	2	3	4	5
MM					
MM+acetylornithine					x
MM+ornithine	x				x
MM+citrulline	x	x			x
MM+argininosuccinate	x	x	x		x

If the 5 types of E. coli listed in Table 2, all types that were able to grow on MM + ornithine were also able to grow on MM + acetylornithine EXCEPT:

A: Type 1

B: Type 2

C: Type 3

D: Type 5

Always be careful of questions with "EXCEPT" or "NOT" in them; it's very easy to get confused or forgetful and answer the question incorrectly.

The information accompanying Table 2 states that E. coli can grow on a medium if there is an "x" in the corresponding cell. The question is looking for the E. coli type that can grow on MM + ornithine but not MM + acetylornithine (remember the "EXCEPT"!). This means we're looking for the E. coli type with an x in the MM + ornithine cell but no x in the MM + acetylornithine cell.

Looking at the table, types 2 and 3 don't have x's for either MM + ornithine or MM + acetylornithine, so they're incorrect. Type 5 has an x for both, so it's also incorrect. However, type 1 has an x for MM + ornithine but not for MM + acetylornithine. Type 1 is the only type that can grow on MM + ornithine but not MM + acetylornithine, so answer choice A is correct.

This question is a bit trickier because the experiment is somewhat confusing and the question includes "EXCEPT," but you still follow the same process of looking at the visual(s) to find the correct answer.

Interpreting Trends Questions

Interpreting trends questions are all about figuring out how variables within a figure relate to each other or how different figures in a passage relate to each other.

You may need to analyze how different variables relate to each other or put data in increasing or decreasing order based on some criteria like height or mass and make interpretations from there. To answer interpreting trends questions, it's useful to know the different relationships variables can have. Below is a brief summary of the three main types of variable relationships.

Direct Correlation: For direct correlation, the variables move in the same direction. As one variable increases, so does the other variable, OR as one variable decreases so does the other variable. One direct relationship is height vs age in children. As a child's age increases, so does his/her height.

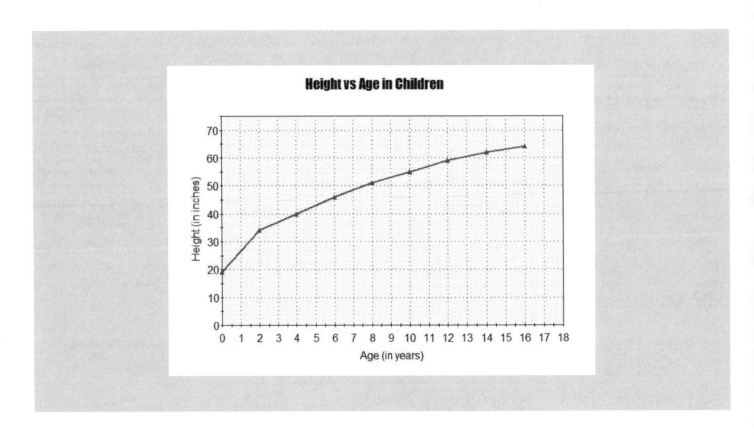

Inverse Correlation: This is the opposite of direct correlation. As one variable increases, the other variable decreases, and vice
versa. Shopping is a simple example: as you purchase more items, the amount of money you have decreases.

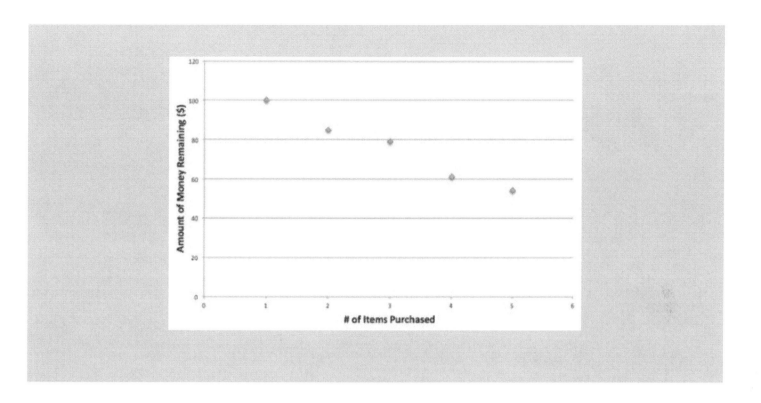

No Clear Relationship: Sometimes there is no clear relationship between the variables. Here is a graph of data with no direct or inverse relationship. If you try to describe this relationship in one word, you can't. As you follow the trend, as temperature increases, density increases, but then it starts to decrease rapidly. So temperature and density are not inversely or directly related.

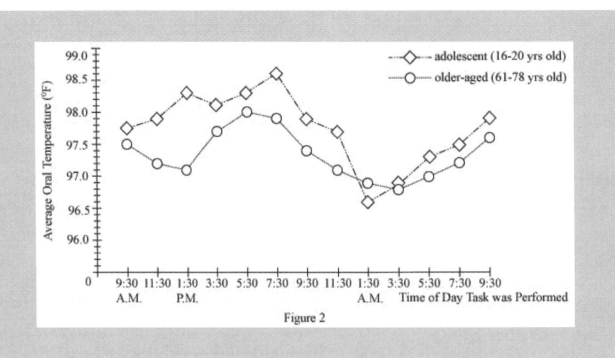

Figure 2

Try this sample interpreting trends question:

Soils are composed of mixtures of differently sized particles. Soils can be classified by texture (the composition of the soil based on proportions of sand, silt, and clay particles) and porosity (percent of a soil's total volume composed of open space). Table 1 shows soil particle types with their typical diameters. A well sorted soil is composed of particles with low variation in diameter, while a poorly sorted soil is composed of particles with wide variation in diameter.

Table 1	
Particle Category	Particle Diameter (mm)
Gravel	> 2.0
Very Coarse Sand	1.1-2.0
Coarse Sand	0.6-1.0
Medium Sand	0.26-0.5
Fine Sand	0.14-0.25
Very Fine Sand	0.07-0.13
Silt	0.004-0.06
Clay	< 0.004

Study 1

A 500g sample a soil (Soil 1) was washed through a screen with 0.06mm holes to remove all clay and silt particles. The soil remaining on the screen was dried and weighed, then sifted through a series of screens with progressively smaller holes to separate particles of different categories. The particles collected for each category were then weighed. This procedure was repeated for samples of 4 other soils (Soils 2-5). Table 2 shows the results of this study.

Table 2					
	Weight (g) of Particles				
Particle Category	Soil 1	Soil 2	Soil 3	Soil 4	Soil 5
Gravel	0	0	0	0	36
Very Coarse Sand	0	132	0	0	54
Coarse Sand	0	241	0	0	197
Medium Sand	0	127	35	134	76
Fine Sand	14	0	136	245	36
Very Fine Sand	11	0	79	96	33

Study 2

A sample was taken from each of Soils 1-5 and dried by heating at 101°C for 24 hours, and was then weighed. Table 3 shows the calculated porosity and the void ratio (ratio of the volume of open space to the volume of solid material) of each soil sample.

Table 3		
Soil	Porosity (%)	Void Ratio
1	45	0.82
2	34	0.52
3	43	0.75
4	42	0.72
5	10	0.11

Based on the combined results of Studies 1 and 2, a researcher concludes that there is an inverse relationship between particle diameter and porosity. Is this claim supposed by the data in Tables 2 and 3?

A: Yes, because as the average diameter of particles in a sample decreases, the porosity increases

B: Yes, because as the average diameter of particles in a sample increases, the porosity increases

C: No, because as the average diameter of particles in a sample decreases, the porosity increases

D: No, because as the average diameter of particles in a sample increases, the porosity increases

This question wants to know if there is an inverse relationship between particle diameter and porosity, and it's asking you to look at Tables 2 and 3 to find out. As a reminder, in an inverse relationship, when one variable increases, the other variable decreases.

Table 3 lists the porosity of the different soils, but it's not in any order, so let's list the soils in order of increasing porosity to make it easier to see any trends:

Soil 5: 10% porosity
Soil 2: 34% porosity
Soil 4: 42% porosity
Soil 3: 43% porosity
Soil 1: 45% porosity

Next, we'll look at Table 2 for the different average diameter of particles for each soil. As we can see in Table 1, gravel has the largest average diameter, and clay has the smallest. We don't have time to calculate the exact average particle size for each soil type, so we'll estimate instead by looking at the weight of the different particles for each soil type in Table 3. The higher the weight of a certain particle a soil has, the more of that particle it contains, so soils with lots of sand will have a lower average diameter than soils with lots of gravel. Based on that, here's our list in order of increasing estimated average diameter:

Soil 1 (Smallest average diameter)
Soil 3
Soil 4
Soil 2
Soil 5 (Largest average diameter)

When you're figuring out the correlation trend, don't worry about being absolutely exact with your estimates. We estimated that Soil 5 has the largest average diameter because it's the only soil that contains gravel, and it also contains a significant amount of other particles with large diameters.

Soil 1 has only particles with the smallest diameters (fine sand and very fine sand), so we can estimate it has the smallest average diameter. Soils 3 and 4 seem to have roughly the same average particle size, as do Soils 2 and 5, but even if we were to flip how we ordered those two pairs, we'd still be able to see the general trend between porosity and average diameter below.

Here are our two lists together:

Porosity: Low to High
Soil 5
Soil 2
Soil 4
Soil 3
Soil 1

Particle Size: Low to High
Soil 1
Soil 3
Soil 4
Soil 2
Soil 5

From these lists, we can see that Soil 1 has both the highest porosity and lowest particle size, while Soil 5 has the lowest porosity and highest particle size. The two lists are in roughly opposite order as well, which means this is an inverse relationship: as porosity increases, particle size decreases, and vice versa.

Because it's in inverse relationship, C and D are incorrect. Answer choice B states that, yes, there is an inverse relationship, so you may think it is correct. However, after the "Yes" statement, B describes a direct relationship, not an inverse relationship, so it's incorrect. That means A is the correct answer.

Here's another sample question:

Temperature probes were placed in the apparatus. Figure 2 graphs the change in temperature of M1 and the salt/ice mixture over a period of mixing time.

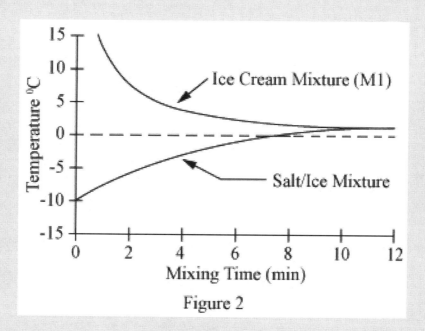

Figure 2

The viscosity (resistance to flow) of an ice cream mixture can be determined by measuring the electrical current drawn by the motor rotating the stirring paddle. Figure 3 shows the change in current over a period of mixing time for M1 and 2 other ice cream mixtures (M2 and M3).

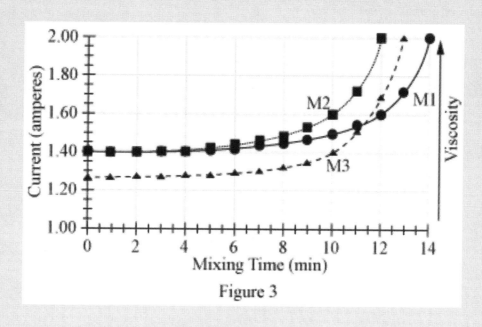

Figure 3

Based on Figures 2 and 3, as the temperature of the ice cream mixture M1 decreased, the viscosity

A: Increased only

B: Decreased only

C: Increased, then decreased

D: Decreased, then increased

This question is trying to determine the relationship between temperature and viscosity. As the temperature of the M1 ice cream mixture decreased, what happened to the viscosity? Looking at Figure 2, we can see that the temperature of M1 decreased steadily from 0 minutes to about 8 minutes, then it began to level off but still decreased slightly. So the more the mixture is mixed, the more its temperature decreases.

In Figure 3, make sure you can see where viscosity is: it's on the y-axis, but on the right side of the graph so you may not notice it immediately. There's no scale for viscosity, but we don't need one since we're not trying to find specific viscosity values; we're just looking for the general pattern. As you move up the y-axis, viscosity increases.

The x-axis of Figure 3 shows mixing time. Since we already determined that the temperature of M1 decreases as mixing time increases, we know that as we move from left to right across the graph, mixing time increases, and the temperature of M1 decreases. That means we want to analyze the M1 plot this direction to see what happens to its viscosity.

Looking at the M1 plot in Figure 3 (the one with the circles), we can see that the viscosity of M1 increases slightly from 0 to about 8 minutes, then it increases sharply. At no point does the viscosity of M1 decrease. This means that A is the correct answer.

Calculations and Estimates Questions

Calculations and estimates questions are the most math-focused Data Representation questions. You'll need to do some basic math in order to answer most of them. Remember, no calculators are allowed on ACT Science, but these calculations are simple enough to do by hand or in your head.

For these questions, you'll need to find a specific value based on information in a figure. If the value you're trying to find is located between values shown in a graph or table then it's an interpolation question, and if it's beyond the range of the data shown it's an extrapolation question.

For example, if a graph shows the temperature of a place from 12:00PM to 8:00PM, an interpolation question could ask a question about the data at, say, 5:00PM, while an extrapolation question could ask about the data at 9:00PM.

Interpolation Questions

For interpolation questions, you'll calculate values that are within the range of the data shown in the figures. They're generally easier than extrapolation questions because all the values are already contained in the visual(s). Here's a sample question:

Table 3

Trial	Concentration of $H_2C_2O_4$ (M)	Reaction Time (sec)
9	0.10	755
10	0.25	541
11	0.50	332
12	0.75	229

Based on the data in Table 3, the reaction time for a $H_2C_2O_4$ concentration of 0.35M is most likely

A: 786 seconds

B: 535 seconds

C: 624 seconds

D: 431 seconds

For this question, we're trying to figure out the reaction time at a concentration of 0.35M. However, 0.35M isn't included in the table which is why we need to interpolate. Taking a quick glance at the table, the relationship between concentration of $H_2C_2O_4$ and reaction time is pretty clear: reaction time decreases as the molar concentration increases.

To solve interpolation questions, you want to identify the two data points on either side of the point you're trying to find, then look for answer choices that are between those two points.

In this question, the points on either side of 0.35M are 0.25M and 0.50M. They have reaction times of 541 seconds and 332 seconds, respectively, so we'll eliminate any answer choices that aren't between those two points. This means crossing off answer choices A and C.

Now we need to decide whether B or D is the correct answer. 0.35M is about midway between 0.25M and 0.50M, so we'd want an answer about midway between 541 and 332 seconds. Answer choice B doesn't fit that requirement because it's much closer to 541 seconds than 332 seconds, but D, 431 seconds, is pretty solidly in the middle. It's the correct answer.

Extrapolation Questions

The other type of Calculations and Estimates question is extrapolation questions. For these questions, you'll need to predict data that is outside the range of what is included in the visual.

Extrapolation questions require identifying a pattern in the data and predicting the next step in that pattern (in whichever direction the question's data lies). These patterns will always be relatively simple, so the steps we take are also relatively simple:

#1: Pinpoint what we're trying to find: is it a value more or less than what we are given in the visual?

#2: Select any two consecutive data points in the table or graph and find the relationship between them. Do they have a direct or inverse correlation?

#3: Use that relationship to predict what the value we're looking for will be.

Try this sample question:

Study 2
A sample was taken from each of Soils 1-5 and dried by heating at 101°C for 24 hours, and was then weighed. Table 3 shows the calculated porosity and the void ratio (ratio of the volume of open space to the volume of solid material) of each soil sample.

Table 3		
Soil	Porosity (%)	Void Ratio
1	45	0.82
2	34	0.52
3	43	0.75
4	42	0.72
5	10	0.11

Based on Study 2, another soil sample that had a void ratio of 0.90 would have had a corresponding porosity closest to:

A: 8%

B: 35%

C: 40%

D: 48%

This is an extrapolation question because the void ratio of 0.90 is beyond the range of the data in the table; it's larger than any of the other void ratios shown. Now we select two consecutive data points from the table and figure out the relationship between porosity and void ratio from them.

Let's choose Soils 1 and 3. Soil 1 has a porosity of 45% and a void ratio of 0.82, and Soil 3 has a porosity of 43% and a void ratio of 0.75. Soil 1 has both a higher porosity and a higher void ratio than Soil 3, so we can conclude that void ratio increases as porosity increases (direct correlation).

Because a void ratio of 0.90 is larger than any void ratio in the table, we can infer that its porosity will also be higher than any porosity in the table, including Soil 1's porosity of 45%.

48% is the only porosity that fits this conclusion, so D is the correct answer.

Recap: Answering Data Representation Questions

Even students who don't feel particularly comfortable running calculations or analyzing charts and graphs can excel on Data Representation questions. This questions often look intimidating since they require you to look at visuals that may be complex, but the majority are pretty straightforward once you understand what's being asked and know which steps to follow.

The main points to remember when answering Data Representation questions are:

- Find the information you're being asked about in the visual and go from there.

- Don't get confused or overwhelmed when looking at complicated visuals. Focus only on the information you're being asked about and ignore everything else.

- Draw lines on graphs if you need to estimate a value.

- If you're answering an extrapolation question and the data you're looking for is beyond the range of the figure, select two consecutive points in the figure and determine the relationship between them, then use that information to estimate the data point you're looking for.

Chapter 9: How to Solve Research Summaries Questions

Like Data Representation questions, Research Summaries questions require you to analyze graphs and tables, but Research Summaries questions will focus more on the different experiments in a passage and how they are similar to/different from each other. Both passages also include fact-finding as well as calculations and estimates questions. We won't go over these two types of questions again again (review Chapter 8 if you'd like a refresher), but don't be surprised if you see them in Research Summaries passages as well as Data Representation passages.

There are two main types of Research Summaries questions: experimental design questions and interpreting experiments questions. In this chapter, we explain each of the Research Summaries questions you may come across and how to answer them.

Experimental Design Questions

The first type of Research Summaries questions we'll discuss are experimental design questions. There are four types of experimental design questions:

- Independent and dependent variable questions
- Comparing and contrasting experiment questions
- Hypothetical changes to the experiment questions
- Why did they do x? questions

These questions will all relate back to the studies you read about in the passage and either the choices scientists made when conducting the study or changes you would make to the study yourself.

Independent and Dependent Variable Questions

Here's a quick recap of what we learned about variables in Chapter 5: In a study, scientists often change experimental variables to observe how the response changes as a result. The variables that scientists actively change are called independent variables. The variables that the scientists then observe are the dependent variables. Here's an example:

Scientist 1 is running an experiment to see how fast a rubber ball rolls down an incline. For each trial of the experiment, Scientist 1 uses different inclines of specific angles. Scientist 1 tested inclines of 10, 25, and 50 degrees. The scientist then timed how fast it took for the ball to roll from the top to the bottom of the incline.

What are the independent and dependent variables here?

The independent variable is what the scientist is controlling/ changing. In this case, Scientist 1 is changing the degree of the incline. The dependent variable is what the scientist is observing. In this case, Scientist 1 is observing how fast the ball rolls down the incline. It's as simple as that!

Scientists might conduct experiments with more complicated scenarios like circuits or heat transfers, but the concept is the same. When data points are on an XY-graph, the independent variable is usually on the x-axis and the dependent variable is usually on the y-axis.

Read through this Research Summaries passage and answer the question that follows it. (Each of the four experimental design sample questions come from this passage.)

In a chemical reaction, the rate expresses the time for the products of the reaction to be generated from the reactants. In the following experiments, a student investigates how different factors affect the rate at which potassium permanganate ($KMnO_4$) is reduced to form manganese (II) ions, carbon dioxide and water after reacting with oxalic acid ($H_2C_2O_4$). As $KMnO_4$ undergoes this reaction it changes in color from purple, to an orange-brown color, and eventually becomes colorless when the reaction is complete.

Experiment 1

A student mixed 15 mL of 1.0 M (moles/liter) $H_2C_2O_4$ in solution with 30 mL sulphuric acid and 60 mL water in a 250 mL beaker. In a separate 100 mL beaker, 15 mL of 0.1 M $KMnO_4$ solution was added. Prior to undergoing any reaction, $KMnO_4$ in solution is purple in color. The two beakers were cooled down to 0°C in an ice bath. The solution of KMnO4 was then added to the second beaker of $H_2C_2O_4$ and sulphuric acid. The time that it took the combined solutions to change color from purple to colorless was recorded. The same protocol was repeated at room temperature (25°) and after warming up both solutions in a water bath of 40°C and 50°C. The results are represented in Table 1.

Table 1

Trial	Temperature (°C)	Reaction Time (sec)
1	0	900
2	25	150
3	40	60
4	50	30

Experiment 2

The same protocol in Experiment 1 was repeated identically, except for that this time a single crystal of manganese sulphate ($KMnO_4$) was added to the solution of $KMnO_4$ prior to mixing with the solution of $H_2C_2O_4$ and sulphuric acid. In this reaction $MnSO_4$ serves as a catalyst. A catalyst is a compound that increases the rate of a reaction but is not consumed in the process. The results from Experiment 2 are shown in Table 2.

Table 2

Trial	Temperature (°C)	Reaction Time (sec)
5	0	282
6	25	52
7	40	28
8	50	14

Experiment 3

Once again the procedure followed in Experiment 1 was repeated, but this time all reactions occurred at room temperature (25°C). In each trial, the concentration of the $H_2C_2O_4$ used varied. The results from Experiment 3 are shown in Table 3.

Table 3

Trial	Concentration of $H_2C_2O_4$ (M)	Reaction Time (sec)
9	0.10	755
10	0.25	541
11	0.50	332
12	0.75	229

In Experiment 1 and 2, as the temperature of the reaction increased, the time for the solution to become colorless:

A: remained the same for Experiment 1 and 2

B: decreased for both Experiment 1 and 2

C: decreased for Experiment 1 and increased for Experiment 2

D: increased for both Experiment 1 and Experiment 2

In this passage, temperature is the independent variable for Experiments 1 and 2 since that is what the scientists are changing, and reaction time (the amount of time for the solution to become colorless) is the dependent variable because that is what changes as a result of manipulating the independent variable. Experiment 2 includes the addition of a crystal of manganese sulfate, but this just serves as another way to change the independent variable.

The question wants to know how an increase in temperature (the independent variable) affected the reaction time (the dependent variable). Looking at Tables 1 and 2, we can see that, as temperature increased, the reaction time decreased in both tables. This means answer choice B is correct.

The passages in ACT Science won't label variables as independent or dependent, so it's up to you to identify them and understand how they affect each other.

Comparing and Contrasting Experiment Questions

Comparing and contrasting experiment questions are another type of experimental design question. For these questions, you'll need to analyze the similarities and differences between two or more experiments.

Here's an example mini-passage:

Scientists wanted to study the impact of different types of gasoline on the mileage of the Toyota Prius Hybrid. In Study 1, each Toyota Prius received a full tank of unleaded gasoline. The car then drove 100 miles on the highway at 55 mph. The amount of remaining gasoline was measured and recorded. In Study 2, each Toyota Prius received a full tank of premium gasoline. The car then drove 100 miles on the highway at 55 mph. The amount of remaining gasoline was measured and recorded.

This question wants to know how Experiments 1 and 3 were different. The best way to answer the question is to go through the answer choices one by one. Starting with A, there is no mention of $MnSO_4$ being added in Experiment 3, and a quick glance at Experiment 2 will tell us $MnSO_4$ was used in that experiment instead. A is false.

For B, we can see in Table 3 that the concentration $H_2C_2O_4$ of changed throughout the trials, so B is also false. Answer choice C is tricky. By reading the first paragraph of the passage, we know that the reaction time for Experiment 3 was measured when the solution became colorless. However, this was true for all the experiments, so it isn't a difference between Experiment 1 and Experiment 3. For answer choice D, it is stated under Experiment 3 that the temperature of the reactions remained constant, and by looking at Table 1 we can see this wasn't true for Experiment 1. Answer choice D is the correct answer.

For Research Summaries passages, you'll almost always be asked at least one question on how the experiments differ from each other, so when you skim the passage the first time, make sure to get a general idea of the main difference(s) between them.

Hypothetical Changes to the Experiment Questions

These questions will ask something like, "Suppose the experiments had been repeated, except instead of _____, the scientists did _____. What would you expect to happen?"

Try this example:

If Experiment 3 were repeated with a solution containing 0.4M of $H_2C_2O_4$, the reaction time would most likely be:

A: greater than 755 sec

B: 600 sec

C: 400 sec

D: less than 229 sec

To answer these types of questions, first you want to understand how the experiment is being changed and what you'll be measuring to determine the change. In this case, the change is using H2C2O4 with a concentration of 0.4M.

Next, we want to understand the impact the change will have. In Table 3, we can see that the experiment was conducted with H2C2O4 at concentrations of 0.10M, 0.25M, 0.5M, and 0.7M. Since 0.4M is between 0.25M and 0.5M, its reaction time will likely be between the reaction times of those two concentrations. The reaction time at 0.25M was 541 seconds, and the reaction time at 0.5M was 332 seconds. Answer choice C, 400 seconds, is the only option between those two values, so it's the correct answer.

Why Did They Do X? Questions

For "why did they do x?" questions you'll be asked why the

scientists decided to make a certain choice in the experiment. Here's an example:

In the three experiments, why was the $KMnO_4$ solution initially put in its own beaker before being added to the $H_2C_2O_4$ and sulphuric acid solution?

A: Because the reaction wouldn't occur if $KMnO_4$ was added immediately to the $H_2C_2O_4$ and sulphuric acid solution.

B: To allow the solutions to reach the correct temperature before starting the reaction.

C: So the crystal of manganese sulphate could be added before the reaction began.

D: To ensure the molar concentrations of $KMnO_4$ and sulphuric acid were accurate.

To answer this question, let's first skim through the passage to see what clues it gives us. There's nothing in the passage that mentions the reaction wouldn't occur if the two solutions were combined right away, so A is incorrect.

From looking at the passage and visuals, we already know that the temperatures of the solutions was a key factor in the experiment since temperature is the independent variable in Experiments 1 and 2, and in Experiment 3 its mentioned that all reactions occurred at 25°C. Additionally, under "Experiment 1" it's stated that the two solutions are cooled or warmed to the appropriate temperature and then added together. That supports answer choice B, but let's quickly look at the remaining two options to make sure of your answer.

The crystal of manganese sulphate was only added in Experiment 2, so it doesn't apply to "the three experiments" as the question states, so C isn't the correct answer either. Answer choice D is also incorrect because, although the scientists likely checked the molar concentrations of the solutions before they were mixed, this was likely done before the experiment started and is never mentioned as a reason the two solutions were not immediately added together.

The means that B is the correct answer.

In most cases, the reason the scientists did "x" was to make the experiment stronger so they can be more sure of accurate results. Scientists really care about bias or messing up the experiment with unintended side effects. In this case, the scientists had to be sure the solutions were at the correct temperature before the reaction began because they were measuring the impact of temperature on reaction time, so they took extra care to get the temperatures of the solutions correct.

Interpreting Experiments Questions

Another type of Research Summaries question is interpreting experiments questions. These questions are similar to experimental design questions in that they ask about the study conducted, but for interpreting experiments questions you'll need to make accurate assumptions about an experiment.

Interpreting experiments questions will give one interpretation of part of the passage and ask you whether that interpretation is true or not. You'll use the data from the experiment to find the correct answer. These questions have a predictable pattern to the question and answers, which you can use to your advantage.

Interpreting experiments questions generally fit one of these templates:

Is the statement "_____" consistent with Figure 1?

A researcher hypothesized "_____." Do the results of Study 2 support that hypothesis?

Answer choices usually follow one of these two formats:

A. Yes, because of [statement 1].
B. Yes, because of [statement 2].
C. No, because of [statement 1].
D. No, because of [statement 2].

OR

A. Yes, because of [statement 1].
B. Yes, because of [statement 2].
C. No, because of [statement 3].
D. No, because of [statement 4].

Here's an example of answer choices from a sample question we'll go over below:

A: Yes, because there are no times where the average oral temperature of the older-aged group is above that of the adolescent group.

B: Yes, because at 1:30AM the average oral temperature of the older-aged group is above that of the adolescent group.

C: No, because there are no times where the average oral temperature of the older-aged group is above that of the adolescent group.

D: No, because at 1:30AM the average oral temperature of the older-aged group is above that of the adolescent group.

As you can see, answer choices A and C are followed by the same statement after the "yes" or "no." The same is true for answer choices B and D. To make it easier to differentiate between the answer choices, you can rewrite them like this:

A: Yes, because Statement 1

B: Yes, because Statement 2

C: No, because Statement 1

D: No, because Statement 2

Where Statement 1 is: There are no times where the average oral temperature of the older-aged group is above that of the adolescent group

Where Statement 2 is: At 1:30AM the average oral temperature of the older-aged group is above that of the adolescent group

Most students who miss these kinds of questions jump the gun by deciding quickly on Yes or No before really looking at the data. As mentioned earlier, answering these questions requires interpreting the data presented in figures and text and deciding whether the data support or contradict the hypothesis.

There are two ways to solve interpreting experiments questions. For one method, you'd first figure out whether the scientist's claim is true or not. If it's true, then you cross off the two answer choices that begin with "No," but if the statement is false, you'd cross off the two answer choices that begin with "Yes." Next, you'd figure out which of the statements is true. Once you know this, you'd cross off the answer choices with incorrect statements, and this will leave you with one answer choice left: the correct answer!

You can also flip the order and first figure out which statement is true, cross off the answer choices that you now know to be wrong, and then determine if the scientist's claim is true or not. Either method works, just use the one you think is easiest for the particular question you're trying to solve.

Try out these questions:

A scientist claims the average oral temperature of the subjects at any time in the adolescent group was always higher than that of the subjects in the older-aged group measured at the same time. Is the claim supported by the date in Figure 2?

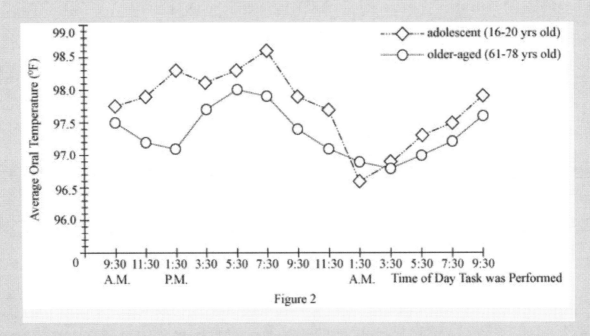

Figure 2

A: Yes, because there are no times where the average oral temperature of the older-aged group is above that of the adolescent group.

B: Yes, because at 1:30AM the average oral temperature of the older-aged group is above that of the adolescent group.

C: No, because there are no times where the average oral temperature of the older-aged group is above that of the adolescent group.

D: No, because at 1:30AM the average oral temperature of the older-aged group is above that of the adolescent group.

First we need to rewrite the answers so that they're easier to understand. There are two main statements in the answer choices: "there are no times where the average oral temperature of the older-aged group is above that of the adolescent group" and "at 1:30AM the average oral temperature of the older-aged group is above that of the adolescent group." We'll call these

Statement 1 and Statement 2, respectively. Now we can rewrite the answer choices with the statement names.

A: Yes, because Statement 1

B: Yes, because Statement 2

C: No, because Statement 1

D: No, because Statement 2

Statement 1: There are no times where the average oral temperature of the older-aged group is above that of the adolescent group

Statement 2: At 1:30AM the average oral temperature of the older-aged group is above that of the adolescent group

We'll next figure out if the scientist's claim is true. Is the oral temperature of the adolescent group always higher than the oral temperature of the older-aged group? Looking at Figure 2, we can see the oral temperature of the adolescent group is the line with the squares, and this line does go below the older-aged group's line at 1:30AM. The scientist's statement is false, so we can cross off answer choices A and B.

Now we decide whether Statement 1 or Statement 2 is true. We just determined that the older-aged group has a higher oral temperature than the adolescent group at 1:30AM, so this means Statement 2 is true, which means the correct answer is D.

Now try a more difficult question:

To survive in a medium (a nutrient system) that lacks arginine (an amino acid), E. coli bacteria must synthesize arginine from the medium. A portion of the reaction pathway to synthesize arginine is shown in Figure 1. Each of these reactions is catalyzed by an enzyme (E1-E4). In the first reaction, E1 catalyzes the conversion of the precursor acetylornithine into the product ornithine. In the second reaction, E2 catalyzes the conversion of the precursor ornithine into the product citrulline.

$$\text{acetylornithine} \xrightarrow{\text{E1}} \text{ornithine} \xrightarrow{\text{E2}} \text{citrulline} \xrightarrow{\text{E3}} \text{argininosuccinate} \xrightarrow{\text{E4}} \text{arginine}$$

Figure 1

Table 1 shows the E. coli genes that code for the enzymes E1-E4.

Table 1	
Gene	Enzyme
arg 1	E1
arg 2	E2
arg 3	E3
arg 4	E4

A gene can be damaged such that it no longer correctly produces its corresponding enzyme. The pathway then stops at the reaction catalyzed by that enzyme. Consequently, the precursor accumulates and the product is not produced. In standard nomenclature, an undamaged gene is labeled with a plus sign (for example, arg^{1+}). A damaged gene that cannot produce its enzyme is labeled with a minus sign (for example, arg^{1-}).

Experiment

A biologist grew wild-type (naturally occurring) E. coli on minimal medium (MM), a medium that does not contain arginine.

The biologist then irradiated the E. coli to cause genetic damage. Next, she identified E. coli that could no longer synthesize arginine in MM. She created five variations of media and tested these E. coli on each media to observe growth. Table 2 shows classification of E. coli into 5 types depending on the media on which they grew. An "x" indicates that a given type could grow on the corresponding medium and therefore could synthesize arginine from that medium.

Table 2					
	Type				
Medium	1	2	3	4	5
MM					
MM+acetylornithine					x
MM+ornithine	x				x
MM+citrulline	x	x			x
MM+argininosuccinate	x	x	x		x

A scientist claims that Type 1 E. coli is most likely arg1$^-$ arg2$^+$ arg3$^+$ arg 4$^+$. Is this claim supported by Table 2?

A: Yes, because arginine is synthesized from MM+ornithine but not MM+acetylornithine.

B: Yes, because arginine is synthesized from MM+acetylornithine but not MM+ornithine.

C: No, because arginine is synthesized MM+ornithine but not MM+acetylornithine

D: No, because arginine is synthesized from MM+acetylornithine but not MM+ornithine.

Again, our first step is to rewrite the answer choices so they're easier to understand. There are two main statements in the answer choices: "arginine is synthesized from MM+ornithine but not MM+acetylornithine" and "arginine is synthesized from MM+acetylornithine but not MM+ornithine." We'll call these Statement 1 and Statement 2, respectively.

A scientist claims that Type 1 E. coli is most likely $arg1^-$ $arg2^+$ $arg3^+$ $arg4^+$. Is this claim supported by Table 2?

A: Yes, because Statement 1

B: Yes, because Statement 2

C: No, because Statement 1

D: No, because Statement 2

Statement 1= arginine is synthesized from MM+ornithine but not MM+acetylornithine

Statement 2 = arginine is synthesized from MM+acetylornithine but not MM+ornithine

First, we'll decide if Statement 1 or Statement 2 is true, and we'll do this by looking at Table 2. Table 2 shows which of the five media E. coli grew on. If a box has an "x" that means E. coli could grow on it and could synthesize arginine from that medium. For this question, we're looking at Type 1 E. coli, so we'll look at the column on the left.

Statement 1 says arginine is synthesized from MM+ornithine but not MM+acetylornithine. From the table, we can see that this is true because the MM+ornithine cell for Type 1 has an x, which shows it can synthesize arginine for Type 1 E. coli. However, the MM+acetylornithine cell doesn't have an x which means it couldn't synthesize arginine for Type 1 E. coli. This means statement 1 is true, so we can cross out answer choices B and D.

Next, we'll figure out if the scientist's claim is true. In the Type 1 column, we can see that MM+acetylornithine doesn't have an x, so arginine wouldn't synthesize. According to the passage, this means that the gene is damaged and can't produced its enzyme (which, for MM+acetylornithine we can see is E1 by looking at Table 1). It's therefore labelled with a minus: $arg1^-$. However, MM+ornithine, MM+citrulline, and MM+argininosuccinate do have x's, so they would be positive. (MM is the control so we're not worrying about it). This means Type 1 E. coli would be $arg1^-$ $arg2^+$ $arg3^+$ $arg4^+$ so the scientist's statement is supported by Table 2. This means we can cross out answer choice C, and we're left with A, which is the correct answer.

Recap: Answering Research Summaries Questions

Research Summaries questions focus on the experiments or studies in a passage. For these questions, you'll need to understand why scientists made certain decisions they did, how different decisions would change the experiment, and how each experiment differs from the others, among other skills. The two main types of Research Summaries questions are experimental design questions and interpreting experiments questions.

There are four kinds of experimental design questions:

1. Independent and Dependent Variables
2. Comparing and Contrasting Experiments
3. Hypothetical Changes
4. Why Did They Do x?

The strategy is the same for all four types of questions:

- Start by figuring out what the question is asking. Which experiment/study is it referring to? What is it asking about? Variables? Hypothetical changes?
- Next, look at the corresponding visuals for help answering the question.
- If you need more information, skim the passage. Start by skimming the experiment or study that the question asks about.
- Skim the rest of the passage if you still haven't found what you are looking for.
- Use process of elimination to help you narrow your focus. Don't be tricked by hidden information.
- Keep digging until you can answer the question.

To solve Interpreting Experiments questions, you need to:

- Break down the answer choices into Yes/No + Statement 1/2(3/4).

- Decide whether Statement 1 or 2 (or 3 or 4) is true. If possible, rule out two answer choices.
- Decide whether the hypothesis/claim in the question is true or false. Rule out any answer choices you now know are incorrect.
- Pick the only remaining answer!

Chapter 10: How to Solve Conflicting Viewpoints Questions

There will only be one Conflicting Viewpoints passage on your ACT Science section, but understanding how to read this passage and answer the questions that follow is still crucial for your ACT score, especially if you're aiming for a top score.

The Conflicting Viewpoints passage is the outlier of the science passages. It doesn't follow the format of the other passages, and it tests you on different skills than they do. In this chapter, we walk you through how to attack this passage and answer each of the question types you'll see on it.

How to Read the Conflicting Viewpoints Passage
As a reminder, the Conflicting Viewpoints passage is different from the other passages you'll see on ACT Science, so we recommend saving this passage for last. This is also the only passage we recommend reading all the way through before you get to the questions since you'll need to have a solid grasp of the student/scientist opinions that are discussed.

Each Conflicting Viewpoints passage will start off with an

introduction which usually gives you some key information about the experiment(s). Then there may be a visual, and finally the passage discusses the opinions of each of the students/scientists.

Timing is important for the entire ACT Science section, but it's especially key for the Conflicting Viewpoints passage. You'll only have about five minutes to spend reading the entire passage and answering about seven questions on it. This doesn't give you any time to waste.

As we mentioned in Chapter 7, when you read the Conflicting Viewpoints passage, you want to think about two key things: what is the main opinion of each of the students/scientists mentioned in the passage and how to these opinions differ from each other? Most students find it helpful to take brief notes as they read the passage so they can quickly refer to them as they answer questions.

Below is a Conflicting Viewpoints passage, followed by the notes we took on it. All the sample questions in this chapter relate to this passage.

In Cycas revoluta (a species of seed plant), males have cones that produce pollen, and females have cones that produce seeds. Pollination requires the movement of pollen from inside a male cone to inside a female cone, where multiple ovules are located and pollinated. The ovules then develop into seeds. Below, two students discuss this pollination process.

Experiments

The students proposed 3 experiments using a Cycas revoluta population in an area with sap beetles and in which the percentage of ovule pollination in normally 99% (see table).

Experiment	Procedure
1	Some female *Cycas revoluta* cones are covered with plastic bags that exclude insects and wind.
2	Some female *Cycas revoluta* cones are covered with mesh bags that exclude insects, but not wind.
3	Some female *Cycas revoluta* cones are covered with cylinders that exclude wind, but not insects.

Student 1

In Cycas revoluta, 80% of ovule pollination results from insect pollination, and 20% results from wind pollination. These are the only two pollination mechanisms.

Cycas revoluta have mutually beneficial relationships with certain species of insects. Sap beetles swarm male Cycas revoluta cones when these cones are releasing pollen. When they enter the cones, the sap beetles become covered with the plant's pollen. The sap beetles then visit the female Cycas revoluta cones and deposit some of the pollen when it rubs off them. In the absence of sap beetles, the percent of ovule pollination in Cycas revoluta is about 20%.

Wind pollination is infrequent because Cycas revoluta pollen is large and heavy, making it difficult for it to travel long distances by wind. Additionally, the openings in the female cones are aligned horizontally, so wind-borne pollen must be blown horizontally in order to enter these cones.

Student 2

Wind pollination causes the majority, about 90%, of Cycas revoluta pollination, while only about 10% of ovule pollination in Cycas revoluta is caused by insects. Without wind pollination, the percent of ovule pollination decreases by 90%. If neither of these processes occur, the percent of ovule pollination decreases by 100%.

Wind tunnel experiments show that the shape of the female Cycas revoluta cones creates air currents that facilitate the horizontal movement of pollen into these cones so it is easier for windborne pollen to enter. Additionally, male Cycas revoluta cones produce enormous quantities of pollen, a trait that is common only in wind-pollinated plants. This means the majority of pollen can miss the female cones and the cones will still be pollinated because so much pollen is carried by the wind.

Pollination by sap beetles is infrequent because the beetles prefer other plant species over Cycas revoluta and only rarely visit Cycas revoluta, minimizing the amount of pollination they can perform.

Key info from the passage:
- Student 1 believes majority of pollination is from insects
- Student 2 believes majority of pollination is from wind
- Ways Student 1's and Student 2's beliefs are similar: wind and insect pollination are the only types of pollination for this plant species.

- Ways Student 1's and Student 2's beliefs are different: Student 1 believes the most pollination is from insects and that wind pollination is rare because the pollen is heavy and the openings of the female cones make it hard for windblown pollen to enter. Student 2 believes most pollination is from wind and pollination by beetles is rare because sap beetles only rarely visit this species.

It'll take some trial and error for you to figure out how many notes you should take to have a good grasp of the passage but still have enough time to answer the questions. Your notes don't always need to be as in-depth as those above, especially if you're pressed for time. Even just writing "insects" next to Student 1 and "wind" next to Student 2 can help you keep their opinions straight when answering questions.

Conflicting Viewpoints Question Types
There are three types of questions you'll see in the Conflicting Viewpoints passage: understanding viewpoints, comparing viewpoints, and fact-based.

Understanding Viewpoints Questions
Understanding viewpoints questions focus on analyzing the opinion of just one of the scientists/students discussed in the passage. They commonly include one or more of the following phrases:

- "What would Scientist 1 predict to happen?"
- "Scientist 1 would most likely agree with"
- "Which statement most agrees with Scientist 1's hypothesis?"

To answer these questions, first make sure you're looking at the correct scientist/student opinion. You're only focusing on one opinion in these questions, so ignore the others in the passage. Some understanding viewpoints questions are as easy as finding the fact in the passage, while others will require more logic or analysis.

When answering these questions, remember to ignore the validity of the viewpoint mentioned in the question. Sometimes one viewpoint will be factually false, and you will know it from your previous science studies. Don't worry about this. You should only concentrate on the information in the passage and what it says is true and false.

Below are two sample understanding viewpoints questions.

Student 1 would most likely agree with the statement that Cycas revoluta pollen is:

A: never present in male Cycas revoluta cones

B: produced in the female Cycas revoluta cones

C: smaller than the pollen found in most plants

D: not carried long distances by the wind

This question is asking about Student 1, so let's go back to our notes and see what we jotted down for Student 1's opinion. Student 1 believes about 80% of Cycas revoluta pollination is due to insects and about 20% is due to wind.

For many Conflicting Viewpoints questions, including this one, you'll likely need to go back and review parts of the passage in order to eliminate answer choices. Starting with answer choice A, we know it's incorrect because Student 1 mentions sap beetles becoming covered in pollen from male Cycas revoluta cones.

B is incorrect because Student 1 mentions beetles swarming male cones after those cones have released pollen, not female cones. C is incorrect because Student 1 states that the pollen is "large and heavy."

As for answer choice D, Student 1 states that it's "difficult" for Cycas revoluta pollen to be carried long distances by wind and believes only about 20% of Cycas revoluta pollination is caused by wind. They believe wind pollination is difficult and the pollen is large and heavy, so this is a statement they would agree with. D is the correct answer.

Suppose the three experiments were performed as described. Student 2's hypothesis would be best supported if the percentages of ovule pollination were the roughly the same for which of the following two groups of female Cycas revoluta cones?

A: Those in Experiment 1 that were covered with plastic bags and those in Experiment 1 that were not covered with plastic bags.

B: Those in Experiment 1 that were covered with plastic bags and those in Experiment 2 that were covered with mesh bags.

C: Those in Experiment 2 that were covered with mesh bags and those in Experiment 2 that were not covered with mesh bags.

D: Those in Experiment 2 that were covered with mesh bags and those in Experiment 3 that were covered with cylinders.

From our skimming, we know that Student 2 believes that nearly all of Cycas revoluta pollination is due to wind. The table shows that covering cones in plastic bags prevents both wind and insect pollination, covering them in mesh bags prevents insect but not wind pollination, and covering them with cylinders prevents wind but not insect pollination.

If it helps, you can rewrite the answer choices with the types of pollination that would be possible:
A: none vs wind and insect
B: none vs wind
C: wind vs wind and insect
D: wind vs insect

Student 2 states that 90% of Cycas revoluta pollination is from wind pollination, 10% is from insects, and those are the only two ways this species is pollinated. You can then substitute the pollination types with the percentage of pollination Student 2 thinks would occur to see which option has two groups with the most similar numbers. So wind would be 90%, insect 10%, both types 100%, and neither 0%:

A: 0 vs 100
B: 0 vs 90
C: 90 vs 100
D: 90 vs 10

Answer choice C has the two groups with the closest numbers. This makes sense since, because Student 2 believes so little pollination occurs from insects, they believe cones exposed to both wind and insect pollination would have about the same pollination rate as cones exposed to just wind pollination. C is the correct answer.

Comparing Viewpoints Questions

Comparing viewpoints questions ask about more than one of the scientist/student opinions. You'll need to identify similarities or differences between the authors.

Comparing viewpoints questions may include phrases like:
- "Scientist 1 and 2 agree that…"
- "Which of the following statements would support Scientist 1 but not Scientist 2?"

These questions will often require more analysis compared to understanding viewpoints questions since you'll need to

Based on the experiments described in the table, Students 1 and 2 would most likely agree that the percent of ovule pollination would be highest in female Cycas revoluta cones that are:

A: covered with plastic bags that block wind and insects

B: not covered with a bag or cylinder

C: covered with mesh bags that block insects

D: covered with cylinders that block wind

To answer this question, we need to recall the facts Student 1 and Student 2 agreed on and the facts they disagreed on. Student 1 believes the majority of Cycas revoluta pollination is from insects while Student 2 believes it's from wind. This means Student 1 wouldn't agree with answer choice C, and Student 2 wouldn't agree with answer choice D; so they're both out.

Answer choice A is incorrect because both students agree wind and insects are the only methods of pollination, and if the cones were covered in plastic bags, there'd be no pollination at all. This means B is the correct answer since uncovered cones can experience both wind and insect pollination.

Student 1 states that "wind-borne pollen must be blown horizontally to enter these cones." Which of the following describes how Student 2 responds to this statement? Student 2 argues that the shape of the:

A: female Cycas revoluta cones creates air currents that decrease the likelihood that pollen will enter the cones.

B: female Cycas revoluta cones create air currents that increase the likelihood that pollen will enter these cones.

C: male Cycas revoluta cones create air currents that decrease the likelihood that pollen will enter the cones.

D: male Cycas revoluta cones create air currents that increase the likelihood that pollen will enter the cones.

Again, we know that Student 1 thinks that the majority of Cycas revoluta pollination is from insects and Student 2 thinks the majority is from wind. So Student 2 will believe that it's easier for wind-borne pollen to enter the cones.

From the passage, we know that the pollen enters female cones, so we can immediately cross off answer choices C and D since they discuss male cones. Now we're down to A and B. Answer choice A references decreasing the likelihood pollen will enter the cones, which doesn't fit Student 2's belief that wind pollination is frequent in Cycas revoluta, so it's incorrect. However, B mentions currents that increase the likelihood pollen will enter the female cones. This supports Student 2's opinion, so it's the correct answer.

For most questions on the Conflicting Viewpoints passage, you'll need to analyze the opinions of the students/scientists mentioned in the passage. However, sometimes there will be one question that is a straight fact-based question, similar to those you'd see in Research Summaries or Data Representation passages.

Here's an example:

Which of the following would most likely be used as a control group for Experiment 3?

A: Male Zamia cones covered with cylinders

B: Male Zamia cones left uncovered

C: Female Zamia cones covered with cylinders

D: Female Zamia cones left uncovered

You don't need to worry about the opinions of the students for this question; you just need to know the facts of the experiment and have some logic. The control group is the group left unchanged so the researchers have something to compare all the changes they made in the experiment to. This means it would have to be one of the options of cones left uncovered, since that is their natural state. So it's either B or D. In the table, we can see that it's the female cones that are covered by mesh bags or cylinders, which means the students would need a control for the female cones since they're the ones being affected. That makes D the correct answer.

Recap: Answering Conflicting Viewpoints Questions

Even though there will only be one of them on ACT Science, the Conflicting Viewpoints passage can be intimidating because it doesn't follow the format of any of the other passages in the section.

There are three types of questions on the Conflicting Viewpoints passage: fact-finding questions, understanding viewpoints, and comparing viewpoints. You'll answer fact-finding questions like many questions you see in other passages: just select the answer choice best supported by information in the passage. For understanding viewpoints and comparing viewpoints questions, you'll need to understand and sometimes analyze the viewpoints of one or more of the students/scientists discussed in the passage. For these questions, remember to always make sure you're looking at the correct opinion, and don't get caught up in the validity of a particular opinion/argument.

There are several key things to remember when working on the Conflicting Viewpoints passage:
- Save it for last regardless of its order in the section.
- Read the entire passage before you tackle the questions.
- Jot down important notes on the opinions of students/scientists and how they differ.
- Be especially aware of your time management during this passage since its longer than the other passages and you won't be able to just skim it.

Chapter 11: ACT Study Tips

Now you have all the information you need to ace ACT Science, but you still need to sit down and put some studying in. Studying effectively will save you hours of time and help you get a higher score than studying without goals or strategies.

This chapter discusses 12 of the best ACT study tips, to take you from the time you try your first practice question right up through test day. These tips will help you create an efficient, personalized study plan that'll help you eliminate your weak areas and reach your ACT Science goal score.

#1: Create a Study Schedule

There are probably dozens of things you'd rather do than study for ACT Science, so it's easy for studying to get pushed to the bottom of your to-do list and not happen as often as it should. One of the best ways to avoid this is to develop a set study schedule and stick to it. A study schedule lets you plan out ahead of time when you'll study for ACT Science, which can make it more likely that you get the studying in that you need to.

Try to set aside a regular time to study ACT Science each day or week, such as weekdays from 8:00-9:30 or Sundays from 12:00-4:00. Doing so will make it easier to study because you'll know ahead of time when you should be studying and can fit the rest of your schedule around it.

You should only cancel your study session if you absolutely have to, and in those cases you should set up an alternate time to study to make sure you're getting in the study hours you need.

#2: Practice, Practice, Practice

Reading about the types of questions you'll see on ACT Science and getting tips on how to attack them is important to getting a good score, but answering practice questions will be the most critical part of your ACT Science studying.

By taking practice tests and answering practice questions, you'll get firsthand experience of what ACT Science questions are like, figure out where your strengths and weaknesses are, and learn how well you're currently scoring on ACT Science. We recommend completing individual practice questions, complete Science sections, and full ACTs. During your study period, your goal should be to take at least three complete ACTs, spaced evenly throughout your studying, and seven to eight practice ACT Science sections so you really become an expert at this section.

As often as possible, you should take the entire practice

test/Science section in one sitting and with correct timing. It may be tempting to just answer a few questions here and there or take as long as you want answering questions, but this isn't the best way to study. You need to see how well you score when taking a long test with time constraints so you can get an accurate idea of how well you're scoring.

Additionally, even if you're mainly focusing on the science section of the ACT, be sure to take at least a few complete practice exams. One of the reasons ACT Science is so difficult is that it comes at the very end of the exam, and you'll want to know ahead of time how well you do on this section after several hours of testing. If you find you're especially tired by the time you get to ACT Science and that causes you to answer questions slower or make careless mistakes, you can take steps to correct those problems (by practicing more) before exam day.

#3: Supplement Your Studying With Official Practice Questions

No matter how many practice questions you answer, it won't help your score if the questions you're using are low quality. You want to make sure the practice questions you study with give you an accurate idea of what to expect on exam day, which means they must be very similar to real ACT Science questions.

All the practice questions in this book were carefully created to have the same format and test the same skills as the questions you'll see on ACT Science. If you're looking for additional practice questions, official ACT practice questions are the one to use. They're made by the same people who make real ACT Science questions, so you can be sure they're accurate.

There are six PDFs of practice ACTs available for free online. You can also buy a print or online version of the Official ACT Prep Guide book, which contains three full-length practice tests and as well as additional practice questions.

#4: Get the Timing Down

The ACT Science section is the tightest time crunch of any section of the test. You'll have 35 minutes to read through seven passages and answer 40 questions. This gives you just over 52 seconds per question.
Practice enough that you can get through each passage in five minutes. It's critical that you're able to do this. If you can't do this in your practice, you won't be able to do it on the day of the exam.

If you're struggling to finish the science section in time, remember to not spend more than a minute on any question and to skim the majority of passages (all except Conflicting Viewpoints) before moving on to the questions. If you continue to run out of time, figure out where that time is being lost. Do you spend a lot of time trying to understand visuals? Look through lots of them on practice questions until you can understand them more quickly. Does a certain question type always slow you down? Practice it until you can answer those questions more easily.

#5: Don't Get Bogged Down With Details

ACT Science passages are full of scientific details that aren't actually needed to answer the questions. This is especially true of charts and graphs. Remember, the ACT purposely makes its visuals look complicated and full of information to confuse you and to mimic what real scientific research looks like. But you aren't reading a science journal – you're answering ACT Science questions.

Trying to understand the entire passage is a huge waste of time because most of the passage isn't going to have a question asked about it, and you don't have time to waste on ACT Science.

What should you do instead? Skim the passage and focus mainly on getting just enough information to answer the following two questions:

- What's the main point here?
- What's the figure showing?

That's it. Just get the gist of what's happening and move on to the questions.

#6: Get Comfortable With Graphs

If you're not comfortable with the complicated graphs you see on ACT Science, it can be difficult to quickly figure out what the important information is.

When looking at graphs, focus first on two things:

- What does each axis of the graph represent?
- What is the main idea the graph is showing?

Look at this example:

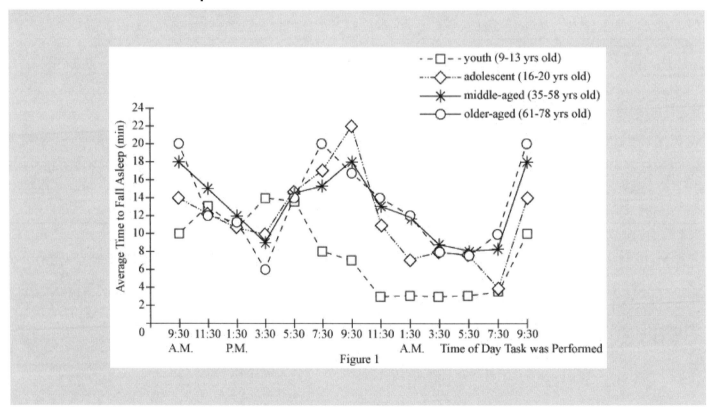

Figure 1

At first glance, this graph looks pretty complicated, but you only need to focus on the main ideas. By looking at the axes, we can see the x-axis shows the time of day and the y-axis shows average time to fall asleep. Each line represents a different age group, so the graph is showing how long various age groups take to fall asleep at different times of the day. That's all you need to understand before moving onto the questions.

For many ACT Science questions, you only need this sort of basic information to answer all the questions about a particular graph. Practice is the best way to become comfortable with complicated-looking graphs so, again, be sure you're studying regularly for ACT Science.

#7: Review and Redo Every Question You Get Wrong

Even once you've taken a practice ACT Science section and graded your answers, your work isn't quite over. You now need to review every question you got wrong, as well as the questions you just happened to guess correctly on but don't really understand how to solve.

This task can be time consuming and frustrating, so it's easy to just skip it and tell yourself that you'll get those questions right the next time you take a practice test. However, it's extremely important you don't do sp. Many, many students take the ACT multiple times each year and get the same score time after time. This isn't surprising when you consider that many of them do little to no studying in between tests. This means they don't learn from their mistakes, repeat those mistakes on subsequent exams, and essentially throw time and money out the window with every additional ACT they take. Don't let this be you.

Reviewing and redoing the questions you got wrong is the most important step in your ACT Science studying. It's by doing this that you'll learn what your strengths and weaknesses are and how you can stop making the same mistakes over and over.

What are some common reasons that you missed a question? Don't just say, "I didn't get this question right." Always take it one step further: what specifically did you miss, and what do you need to improve for the future?

Here are some examples of common reasons you miss an ACT Science question, and how you take the analysis one step further:

Content: I didn't have the science knowledge to understand what was being described in the passage. Example: "I forgot how forces work in physics."

One step further: What specific content do I learn, and how will I learn this? How could I have done better, even without understanding the passage?

Incorrect Approach: I understood the passage, but I didn't know how to solve this question. Example: "I didn't know how to extrapolate the line in the graph."

One step further: How do I solve the question? Where have I seen other questions like this? How will I similar questions in the future?

Careless Error: I misread what the question was asking for or solved for the wrong thing. Example: "I confused Scientist 2's perspective with Scientist 1's."

One step further: Why did I misread the question? What should I do in the future to avoid this?

Get the idea? You're really digging into understanding why you're making every single mistake. Yes, this is hard and it takes work. That's why most students who study ineffectively don't improve.

When you're reviewing questions you got wrong the first thing you probably do is read the answer explanation and think about it a little. This is too easy. It's passive learning, and you're not actively engaging with the mistake you made.

Instead, try something different - find the correct answer choice (A-D or F-J), but don't look at the explanation. Instead, try to resolve the question and get the correct answer.

This will often be hard. You couldn't solve it the first time, so why could you solve it the second time around? But this time, with less time pressure, you might spot a new strategy, or something else will pop up. Something will just "click" for you.

When this happens, what you learned will stick with you far better than if you just read an answer explanation. Because you've struggled with it and reached a breakthrough, you retain that information significantly better than if you just passively absorbed the information.

It's too easy to just read an answer explanation and have it go in one ear and out the other. You won't actually learn from your mistake, and you'll make that mistake over and over again. Treat each wrong question like a puzzle. Struggle with each wrong answer for up to ten minutes. Only then if you don't get it should you read the answer explanation.

#8: Create New Questions for Those You Missed

Missed questions are such important learning opportunities that we have another strategy for getting the most out of them. This is an especially good strategy for questions you're really struggling with or getting wrong repeatedly. After you fully review the question and understand exactly why you missed it, create two more questions yourself in the same style. Then solve them.

These questions that you make are meant to be close replicas of the original question so that they test the same skill with the same passage but use slightly different scenarios.

If it's a graph-related question, change the numbers so you're looking at a different part of the graph.

If it's about conflicting viewpoints, change which scientist you're talking about.

This is great practice for ACT Science because the questions are so stylistically formulaic, which makes it a lot easier to create realistic questions.

What do you gain from doing this? You'll give yourself more chances to practice the very question you just missed. This gives you instant reinforcement of your weakness. Think of it this way, if a professional football player was giving you advice on how to throw the perfect spiral, would you only throw the ball once and then stop, figuring that was enough practice? Of course not! You'd throw the ball multiple times, each time getting more advice and improving a little bit more.

The same is true of the ACT, and especially ACT Science. If you instantly practice right after noticing a weakness, you'll get rid of your weakness far more quickly.

Additionally, when you follow this tip you put yourself in the mind of the exam makers which helps you understand how the ACT is constructed. This can help you spot tricks the exam makers use.

Here's a question from the visual we saw in tip #6:

Based on Figure 1, at which of the following times was the average time to fall asleep most different for the middle-aged and older-aged age groups?

Some simple changes you could make to this question are:

- Find which times the average time to fall asleep was most similar for middle-aged and older-aged groups.
- Find which times the average time to fall asleep was most different for two different groups (for example youth and middle-aged or adolescent and older-aged).

Here's an example from a Conflicting Viewpoints passage:

> Based on the experiments described in the table, Students 1 and 2 would most likely agree that the percent of ovule pollination would be highest in female Cycas revoluta cones that are:

Change you could make to this question are:

- Figure out what Students 1 and 2 would most likely disagree about.
- Find what Students 1 and 2 would most likely agree about the percent of ovule production that would be lowest in female cones.

#9: Figure Out Where You Need to Make Improvements

Every time you complete a practice ACT Science section, make note of how many questions you got wrong each for Data Representation, Research Summaries, and Conflicting Viewpoints passages.

Can you spot any trends? For example, you may do well on Data Representation and Research Summaries passages but struggle with Conflicting Viewpoints passages. Next, go one step further. Which questions in the Conflicting Viewpoints passages do you struggle with the most? Comparing viewpoints, where you need to understand multiple opinions? Fact-based questions since the answer to these is often a minor detail in the passage?

#10: Drill Your Weaknesses

One of the best ways to increase the effectiveness of your studying is to accurately pinpoint where you need to make the most improvements, and then focus your studying on those areas.

Once you've figured out where your weaknesses are in ACT Science, target those areas in your studying. Reread the chapters in this book that discuss those particular question types if you need to remind yourself of the correct strategies to use. Find lots of sample questions of those problems and answer them, carefully making note of where you're making mistakes.

Many students make the mistake of studying all question types equally, but if you already understand how to answer certain question types, you're wasting valuable study time going over them again when you won't learn anything from it. Figure out what your weaknesses are and make them a priority in your studying.

#11: Eliminate Careless Mistakes

Even if you know every skill and strategy you need to ace ACT Science, you may still make careless mistakes. Making these mistakes can be incredibly frustrating because you understand the question but you got excited or distracted and slipped up. It can be as simple as being asked about Scientist 2 but answering for Scientist 1 instead.

ACT Science has a few especially tricky question types that are designed to confuse you. If you understand this beforehand and know how to defeat them, you're less likely to get them wrong.

The first type is the interpreting experiments question from a

Research Summaries passage. The answer choices for this question type are almost always in this form:

- No, because A
- No, because B
- Yes, because A
- Yes, because B

Here's an example:

A scientist claims the average oral temperature of the subjects at any time in the adolescent group was always higher than that of the subjects in the older-aged group measured at the same time. Is this claim supported by the data in Figure 2?

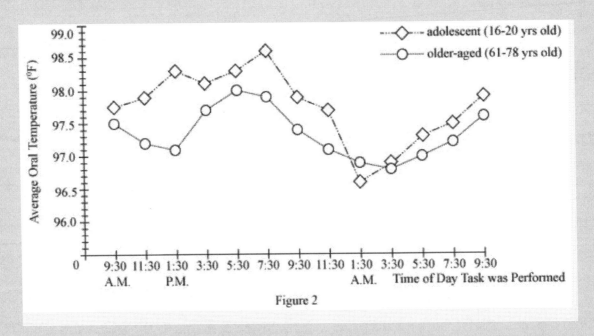

Figure 2

A: Yes, because there are no times where the average oral temperature of the older-aged group is above that of the adolescent group.

B: Yes, because at 1:30AM the average oral temperature of the older-aged group is above that of the adolescent group.

C: No, because there are no times where the average oral temperature of the older-aged group is above that of the adolescent group.

D: No, because at 1:30AM the average oral temperature of the older-aged group is above that of the adolescent group.

(The answer to this question is D.)

The tricky part to these questions is that you can focus on getting one half right and then miss the other half.

For example, you might focus so much on verifying if the claim is true or not that you pick answer choice C, which is correct in stating the claim is false, but incorrectly states that there was no time when the older-aged group had a higher average temperature than the adolescent group.

To combat this, answer each half independently.

First, is this claim supported by the data in Figure 2? No, because there are times when the older-aged group had a higher average temperature than the adolescent group. This means you can eliminate choices A and B.

Next, why is the claim not supported? The claim isn't supported because, at 1:30AM, the average oral temperature of the older-aged group is above that of the adolescent group. That eliminates C, leaving only D left.

Make sure both parts of the answer are correct! By splitting the question this way, you're less likely to make a careless mistake by misinterpreting the question.

The other type of question that often causes careless mistakes is comparing viewpoints questions. Conflicting Viewpoints passages will give you the perspectives of two or three scientists, and these questions will ask you about how each one behaves.

Here's an example:

Student 1 states that "wind-borne pollen must be blown horizontally to enter these cones." Which of the following describes how Student 2 responds to this statement? Student 2 argues that the shape of the:

A: female Cycas revoluta cones creates air currents that decrease the likelihood that pollen will enter the cones.

B: female Cycas revoluta cones create air currents that increase the likelihood that pollen will enter these cones.

C: male Cycas revoluta cones create air currents that decrease the likelihood that pollen will enter the cones.

D: male Cycas revoluta cones create air currents that increase the likelihood that pollen will enter the cones.

Here you're tasked with finding the perspective of Student 2, but that can be difficult to remember because the question starts by saying "Student 1" so it's easy to make a mistake.

The correct answer is B, but if you'd accidentally identified Student 1, you would have chosen A and gotten the question wrong.

One way to solve this is to circle the "Student 2" in the question text. Then, when you answer the question, think explicitly in your head, "Student 2 believes that..." You want to avoid considering the wrong perspective.

#12: Set Regular Goals for Yourself

From your first ACT Science study session to your last, you'll want to set regular goals for yourself. You could have daily, weekly, or monthly goals depending on your schedule and what works best for you. The goals could be covering a new topic or increasing your score a certain number of points on a practice exam. Setting goals helps you keep yourself accountable while also giving you an easy way to track your progress and make sure you're on the path to getting the ACT Science score you want, so make sure they're a part of your study plan.

If you're consistently not meeting the goals you set for yourself, you may need to change when you study, how often you study, or the study methods you're using. This might mean making sure your studying is more active rather than passive, such as creating new practice problems for yourself and solving difficult problems without looking at the answer. It could also mean studying more often, removing distractions when you study, or getting a tutor/ purchasing an online program to help you figure out what you need to work on and what the best way to reach your goals is.

At PrepScholar, we have an online prep program that's designed to determine your personal strengths and weaknesses and develop the most effective lesson plan to help you reach your ACT goal score. You can learn more about it by going to www.prepscholar.com/act

Chapter 12: Test Day Tips

Exam day is when you put all the skills and knowledge you learned while studying to the test. If you've read this book through and studied regularly, by the time you sit down to take the ACT you'll know exactly what to expect from ACT Science and be ready for it. These test day tips will help you recall the information you learned more easily, keep you focused, and give you a smoother test day experience.

General Exam Tips

These tips can be used for the entire ACT Science section, and most of them apply to the rest of the exam as well.

#1: Get a Good Night's Sleep and Eat a Healthy Breakfast Before the Exam

It might sound cheesy, but you'll feel a lot more prepared (and awake) on test day if you get a solid amount of shut-eye the night before the ACT. How many hours you need to feel well rested varies depending on the person, but generally it's good to aim for at least eight hours of sleep.

Heading into test day feeling sleepy and exhausted can dramatically affect your ability to focus and potentially lower your score. So get to bed early!

It's equally important to eat a healthy, filling breakfast before you take the ACT. This way you'll feel more awake and energized before taking the test. What's more, you won't have to worry about a growling stomach later on! Food with protein, such as nuts, eggs, sausage, etc., will help you stay full throughout the test. Also, remember to bring a snack with you to eat during the break between the Math and Reading sections.

#2: Know What to Expect From the ACT and Science Section

Knowing the format of both the science section and the entire ACT will help you be prepared on test day and not get caught off guard by the length or format of the exam.

The ACT is 2 hours and 55 minutes long (175 minutes), or 3 hours and 35 minutes long (215 minutes) if you take the optional essay. Each section is given in one chunk and takes between thirty and sixty minutes. The sections are always in this order:

Subject Area	Total Questions	Time
English	75	45 minutes
Math	60	60 minutes
Reading	40	35 minutes
Science	40	35 minutes
Writing (Optional)	1 essay	40 minutes

You'll get one ten-minute break after the Math section and a five-minute break after the multiple-choice sections if you are taking the essay. Definitely use these breaks to stretch, drink some water, and have a snack.

ACT Science is 35 minutes and contains 40 questions. There will typically be seven passages, divided into three types:

- 3 Data Representation Passages, 5 questions each
- 3 Research Summaries Passages, 6 questions each
- 1 Conflicting Viewpoints Passage, 7 questions

Don't worry about differentiating between Data Representation passages and Research Summaries passages because the strategy you'll use for both is the same. Both of these passages use visuals as the primary way to convey information: there will be graphs, tables, scatterplots, and/or bar graphs.

It's important that you can separate the Conflicting Viewpoints passage from the other two passage types because the strategy for this passage is very different. It should be pretty simple to identify because the Conflicting Viewpoints passage typically has no graphs or tables and includes the opinions of multiple scientists or students.

#3: Pay Attention to Your Timing

Throughout the entire science section, you need to be aware of your timing. Remember, you only have about 52 seconds per question, so spending two or three minutes on a single question without realizing it can really throw you off track.

Practice is key here. By test day you should have a general sense of your pace so the real test doesn't take you by surprise. Be sure to have a rough idea of how long 30 seconds and one minute feel to you when taking practice ACTs. This will help you be a better judge of when you need to move on in the real test environment.

There will usually be a clock in the exam room, but many students like to bring a watch just in case. Just make sure it doesn't beep during the exam, since that is prohibited by the rules. As soon as the section starts, some students will also write down the times they need to finish each passage. So if the science section begins at 11:00AM, you'd jot down a schedule that looks like this:

- Passage 1 finished by: 11:05
- Passage 2: 11:10
- Passage 3: 11:15

#4: Make Sure You're Looking at the Correct Information in the Passage

The most common careless mistake students make during ACT Science is reading the wrong figure or mixing up the labels. If you look at Figure 2 when you're supposed to be looking at Figure 3, you'll make huge mistakes. And you can bet the ACT has trap answers that bait you into these mistakes. Similarly, when you're looking at graphs and tables, you need to make sure you're looking at the correct axis/cell to find the correct data value.

Spend an extra second to two to make sure you're looking at the correct visual or information in a passage; it could seriously help your score!

#5: Use Process of Elimination

When answering questions, process of elimination should be your main strategy for attacking tough or confusing questions. For every ACT Science question there is only one completely correct answer—the rest can be eliminated based on evidence in the passage.

Process of elimination is more foolproof than trying to pick the correct answer out of the pack. Look for reasons to get rid of choices rather than reasons why they might work.

You may have noticed that, for nearly all the answer explanations throughout this book, we solved the problem by eliminating each of the wrong answers until one choice was left instead of just looking for the correct answer. Using this method will help you be more picky about which answer you bubble in, and it will also prevent you from thinking that more than one answer might be correct. If there's even one tiny thing out of place in an answer choice, get rid of it!

#6: Don't Get Stuck on Scientific Terms You Don't Know

As we discussed in Chapter 2, ACT Science is really a misnomer; the test should be called the "reading with very confusing big words and tricky visuals" section. The reason ACT Science doesn't require you to know high-level scientific concepts you might see in AP science classes is that not everyone takes that level of science or math in high school. For ACT Science to be a fair standardized test for all high school students, the test can only ask about basic science concepts. While the questions are often tricky, you won't be need to be familiar with the big science terms it throws at you.

If you need to know a science term to answer a question, the term will be defined for you in the passage. For most of the obscure science terms that are not defined, you will not need to understand them to get to the answer. Think of it as a matching game. For example, if a question asks about average change in AGTB and you do not know what that is, simply find the term "average change in AGTB" in a visual (such as a graph), then see if you can find the data you need to answer the question.

#7: Skip Hard Questions

On ACT Science, time pressure is a very real problem for many students. To avoid losing points, you need to learn to skip questions that are giving you trouble before they eat up too much of your time. Remember, you only have 52 seconds to answer each science question.

As a rule of thumb, if you feel like you're not any closer to figuring out a question after about 30 seconds, move on. Circle that question so that it's easier to spot later on when you want to go back to it. If you're running out of time and still have many questions left, make a quick pass through the whole section and answer all of the easy questions first so you can be sure to get some easy points before the section ends.

#8: Bubble in Your Answers at the End

One easy way to save time on ACT Science (and the rest of the exam) is to wait until the end of the section to bubble in your answers. This cuts down on your time per question by letting you avoid the process of going back and forth between your test booklet and answer sheet. It's more efficient to circle the answers you choose in your test booklet and then fill them in all at once later.

Before using this tip, though, make sure you can reliably finish the section with at least three to five minutes to spare! Don't risk running into a situation in which you don't have enough time to bubble in your answers even though you've gone through all of the questions. Try this method out at least several times during your practice exams before you use it on test day.

#9: Answer Every Question

Since there is no guessing penalty on the ACT, make sure you fill in every bubble! An incorrect answer and an unanswered question both have the same impact on your score (no points gained or lost), so even if you have no idea how to answer a question, it's best to go ahead and guess anyway. You have a 25% chance of getting it right!

#10: Check Your Answers If You Have Extra Time

It's tough to finish ACT Science in time, but if you're able to complete the section with time to spare, go back and check your answers, starting with any questions you skipped or were unsure about (you should circle or mark these questions in some way in your test booklet so you can easily find them again). Sometimes all it takes it a few seconds of review to spot a mistake you made or suddenly understand how to solve a particular problem.

#11: Stay Calm

The most important thing to remember throughout the ACT is to keep a cool head. Especially given the time pressure, students who suffer from test anxiety often stress out if they have to skip a few questions. Don't let this happen to you! Keep moving forward and answer what you can. If you get a question you absolutely have no idea how to answer, skip it and put it out of your mind until you come back to it at the end of the section. You might find questions that initially seemed impossible are much easier when you come back to them. Don't let one question rattle you for the rest of the section.

Tips for Data Representation and Research Summaries Questions

Use these tips for the six Data Representation and Research Summaries passages in the science section.

#12: Skim, Don't Read These Passages

Since every question is worth the same point value and you only have about 52 seconds per question, you want to answer as many questions as you can in the shortest amount of time. One of the best ways to do this is to just skim the Data Representation and Research Summaries passages, rather than read them straight through.

Most of the questions in these two types of passages can be answered by using the visuals and not reading the passage, so you will actually save time and answer more questions correctly by just skimming the actual passages.

#13: Rely Primarily on the Visuals

The ACT Science section hits you with a lot of complicated terminology and unfamiliar facts that make it seem overwhelming. The best policy when faced with all of this information is to ignore most of the information in the passage and focus mainly on the graphs or tables. They should provide enough information for you to answer the majority of the questions you're faced with.

Don't be intimidated by complicated visuals either. Remember to just focus on the axes of a graph or labels of a table as well as the main point of what a visual is showing. You won't need the majority of information a visual is showing to answer the questions.

Tips for Conflicting Viewpoints Questions

Use these tips for the one Conflicting Viewpoints passage in the science section.

#14: Save the Conflicting Viewpoints Passage for Last

Again, every question in the ACT Science section has the same point value, and you want to get the most points in the limited amount of time given. To do this, you should save the most time-consuming passage for last, which is Conflicting Viewpoints.

The Conflicting Viewpoints passage usually has no graphs or tables. Instead, there are two or more scientist or student theories presented in short paragraphs. The questions ask you about each viewpoint and the differences and similarities between the viewpoints. You need to read and understand the entire passage to answer the questions. This passage will take the longest, so save it for last so it doesn't kill your pace.

#15: Write a Mini-Summary of the Passage

Writing summaries will help you remember what each scientist or student argued and will help you when answering the questions. These summaries should be short and give show just the main idea of each opinion. Here's an example of some very brief notes:

Student 1

In *Cycas revoluta*, 80% of ovule pollination results from insect pollination, and 20% results from wind pollination. These are the only two pollination mechanisms.

Cycas revoluta have mutually beneficial relationships with certain species of insects. Sap beetles swarm male *Cycas revoluta* cones when these cones are releasing pollen. When they enter the cones, the sap beetles become covered with the plant's pollen. The sap beetles then visit the female *Cycas revoluta* cones and deposit some of the pollen when it rubs off them. In the absence of sap beetles, the percent of ovule pollination in *Cycas revoluta* is about 20%.

Insect pollination

Wind pollination is infrequent because *Cycas revoluta* pollen is large and heavy, making it difficult for it to travel long distances by wind. Additionally, the openings in the female cones are aligned horizontally, so wind-borne pollen must be blown horizontally in order to enter these cones.

Student 2

Wind pollination causes the majority, about 90%, of *Cycas revoluta* pollination, while only about 10% of ovule pollination in *Cycas revoluta* is caused by insects. Without wind pollination, the percent of ovule pollination decreases by 90%. If neither of these processes occur, the percent of ovule pollination decreases by 100%.

Wind tunnel experiments show that the shape of the female *Cycas revoluta* cones creates air currents that facilitate the horizontal movement of pollen into these cones so it is easier for windborne pollen to enter. Additionally, male *Cycas revoluta* cones produce enormous quantities of pollen, a trait that is common only in wind-pollinated plants. This means the majority of pollen can miss the female cones and the cones will still be pollinated because so much pollen is carried by the wind.

Wind pollination

Pollination by sap beetles is infrequent because the beetles prefer other plant species over *Cycas revoluta* and only rarely visit *Cycas revoluta*, minimizing the amount of pollination they can perform.

With just those basic notes, you can answer a question like this one:

Student 1 would most likely agree with the statement that Cycas revoluta pollen is:

A: transferred primarily by insects

B: produced in the female Cycas revoluta cones

C: smaller than the pollen found in most plants

D: not carried long distances by the wind

We can see from our notes Student 1 believes most pollination occurs from insects, which means A is the best choice.

For many questions you'll need to know information beyond the basic notes you took, but having them will make it easier for you to remember key information about the passage so you minimize the amount of time you spend rereading it.

Chapter 13: Common ACT Science Mistakes and How to Avoid Them

Even after all of your studying, you'll still likely find yourself making some mistakes on ACT Science. This is normal since it's very hard to eliminate all mistakes on the ACT. However, your goal should be to minimize your weaknesses and trouble areas as much as possible before exam day so you set yourself up for the best score possible.

This chapter explains nine of the most common reasons students make mistakes on ACT Science. For each reason, we go over what the cause is, how you can stop making the mistake, and the chapter(s) in this book you should review if you need a refresher.

#1: Misreading the Visuals

Misreading the visuals is one of the most common ACT Science mistakes. Visuals are such a key source of information in this section, and they contain a lot of information. The most common questions students misread the visuals on are fact-finding questions, calculations and estimates questions, and interpreting experiments questions. Here's an example of a factual question with accompanying graph:

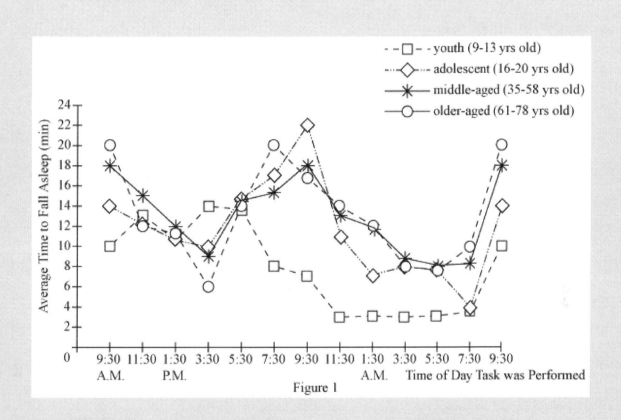

Figure 1

Based on Figure 1, at which of the following times was the average time to fall asleep most different for the middle-aged and older-aged age groups?

A: 3:30 P.M.

B: 7:30 P.M.

C: 9:30 P.M.

D: 1:30 A.M.

This is a pretty straightforward question; all you need to do is see where the largest difference is between the middle-aged and older-aged groups (the correct answer is B). However, there are still many ways to misread the visual. You may end up looking at the wrong lines instead of the middle-aged and older-aged lines, you may accidently find when they are most similar instead of different, you may be looking at it too quickly and find a point when they are different, but not the most different, etc. You also may just be confused by all the lines in the graph and struggle to figure out which points you should be looking at.

If you find yourself not reading graphs, tables, or other visuals correctly, take a step back to figure out why this is happening. Did you not understand the visual, or did you simply make a silly mistake despite knowing what the visual was showing? For the former, work to improve your understanding of graphs and charts by rereading Chapter 4, then work through example problems. Start by not timing yourself on these example problems so you don't feel rushed to understand and complete them.

If you're misreading the visuals because you're going through them too fast and making careless errors, slow down a bit and take a few seconds (less than five is all you need) to reread each question and make sure you're looking at the correct visual and correct part of the visual before you begin answering a question. Understanding visuals is key to doing well on ACT Science, so make sure you feel fully confident in this skill before exam day.

#2: Not Understanding a Trend

This mistake is usually connected to interpreting trends questions and calculations questions in Data Representation passages. They occur when you weren't able to understand or describe the relationship of the data, such as whether it was increasing or decreasing or direct vs indirect.

Here's an example of an interpreting trends question:

Soils are composed of mixtures of differently sized particles. Soils can be classified by texture (the composition of the soil based on proportions of sand, silt, and clay particles) and porosity (percent of a soil's total volume composed of open space). Table 1 shows soil particle types with their typical diameters. A well sorted soil is composed of particles with low variation in diameter, while a poorly sorted soil is composed of particles with wide variation in diameter.

Table 1	
Particle Category	Particle Diameter (mm)
Gravel	> 2.0
Very Coarse Sand	1.1-2.0
Coarse Sand	0.6-1.0
Medium Sand	0.26-0.5
Fine Sand	0.14-0.25
Very Fine Sand	0.07-0.13
Silt	0.004-0.06
Clay	< 0.004

Study 1

A 500g sample a soil (Soil 1) was washed through a screen with 0.06mm holes to remove all clay and silt particles. The soil remaining on the screen was dried and weighed, then sifted through a series of screens with progressively smaller holes to separate particles of different categories. The particles collected for each category were then weighed. This procedure was repeated for samples of 4 other soils (Soils 2-5). Table 2 shows the results of this study.

Table 2					
	Weight (g) of Particles				
Particle Category	Soil 1	Soil 2	Soil 3	Soil 4	Soil 5
Gravel	0	0	0	0	36
Very Coarse Sand	0	132	0	0	54
Coarse Sand	0	241	0	0	197
Medium Sand	0	127	35	134	76
Fine Sand	14	0	136	245	36
Very Fine Sand	11	0	79	96	33

Study 2

A sample was taken from each of Soils 1-5 and dried by heating at 101°C for 24 hours, and was then weighed. Table 3 shows the calculated porosity and the void ratio (ratio of the volume of open space to the volume of solid material) of each soil sample.

Table 3		
Soil	Porosity (%)	Void Ratio
1	45	0.82
2	34	0.52
3	43	0.75
4	42	0.72
5	10	0.11

Based on the combined results of Studies 1 and 2, a researcher concludes that there is an inverse relationship between particle diameter and porosity. Is this claim supposed by the data in Tables 2 and 3?

A: Yes, because as the average diameter of particles in a sample decreases, the porosity increases

B: Yes, because as the average diameter of particles in a sample increases, the porosity increases

C: No, because as the average diameter of particles in a sample decreases, the porosity increases

D: No, because as the average diameter of particles in a sample increases, the porosity increases

This question wants to know if there is an inverse relationship between particle diameter and porosity, and it's asking you to look at Tables 2 and 3 to find out. An inverse relationship would mean that, as particle diameter increases, porosity decreases, and vice versa. To answer this question, you need to be able to see trends in both particle diameter as well as porosity, and you then need to compare the two trends.

To do this, you may need to reorder the tables from greatest to smallest (see Chapter 8 for a step-by-step explanation of how we did this). It should then be clear that there is an inverse relationship between porosity and particle diameter.

If you're struggling with this issue, reread Chapters 4 and 8 and focus on doing a lot of interpreting trends practice problems.

When answering these practice problems, try out different methods to make the trends more clear. This may mean reordering the cells in tables, marking up graphs to see how variables change, and writing the relationship of different variables in your own words so you understand them better.

#3: Not Understanding How an Experiment Is Run

This mistake is usually connected to experimental design questions from Research Summaries passages. It can happen if you didn't understand the researcher's intent, the experiment's design, or what the control, independent, and dependent variables were.

Here's a sample passage and question:

In a chemical reaction, the rate expresses the time for the products of the reaction to be generated from the reactants. In the following experiments, a student investigates how different factors affect the rate at which potassium permanganate ($KMnO_4$) is reduced to form manganese (II) ions, carbon dioxide and water after reacting with oxalic acid ($H_2C_2O_4$). As $KMnO_4$ undergoes this reaction it changes in color from purple, to an orange-brown color, and eventually becomes colorless when the reaction is complete.

Experiment 1

A student mixed 15 mL of 1.0 M (moles/liter) $H_2C_2O_4$ in solution with 30 mL sulphuric acid and 60 mL water in a 250 mL beaker. In a separate 100 mL beaker, 15 mL of 0.1 M $KMnO_4$ solution was added. Prior to undergoing any reaction, $KMnO_4$ in solution is purple in color. The two beakers were cooled down to 0°C in an ice bath. The solution of KMnO4 was then added to the second beaker of $H_2C_2O_4$ and sulphuric acid. The time that it took the combined solutions to change color from purple to colorless was recorded. The same protocol was repeated at room temperature (25°) and after warming up both solutions in a water bath of 40°C and 50°C. The results are represented in Table 1.

Table 1

Trial	Temperature (°C)	Reaction Time (sec)
1	0	900
2	25	150
3	40	60
4	50	30

Experiment 2

The same protocol in Experiment 1 was repeated identically, except for that this time a single crystal of manganese sulphate ($KMnO_4$) was added to the solution of $KMnO_4$ prior to mixing with the solution of $H_2C_2O_4$ and sulphuric acid. In this reaction $MnSO_4$ serves as a catalyst. A catalyst is a compound that increases the rate of a reaction but is not consumed in the process. The results from Experiment 2 are shown in Table 2.

Table 2

Trial	Temperature (°C)	Reaction Time (sec)
5	0	282
6	25	52
7	40	28
8	50	14

Experiment 3

Once again the procedure followed in Experiment 1 was repeated, but this time all reactions occurred at room temperature (25°C). In each trial, the concentration of the $H_2C_2O_4$ used varied. The results from Experiment 3 are shown in Table 3.

Table 3

Trial	Concentration of $H_2C_2O_4$ (M)	Reaction Time (sec)
9	0.10	755
10	0.25	541
11	0.50	332
12	0.75	229

How is the experimental design of Experiment 1 different from that of Experiment 3? In Experiment 3:

A: a crystal of $MnSO_4$ was added as a catalyst

B: the concentration of $H_2C_2O_4$ was constant

C: the reaction time was measured when the solution changed from clear to purple

D: the temperature of the reaction was constant

To answer this question (the correct answer is D), you'll need to be able to understand how Experiment 1 was run, how Experiment 3 was run, and how the two differ from each other. If you misread the passage or just have difficulty understanding experiments, it can be easy to mix key facts up.

For this issue we also recommend slowing down and answering untimed practice science questions before going back to timing yourself. Make sure you read the passage carefully, and then, once you get to a better score, work on the timing. If you still need help figuring out the variables in an experiment or understanding the scientist's intent, reread Chapter 5. In order to understand the experimental design, you need to read the passage carefully, which brings us to the next reason students get questions wrong.

#4: Misreading the Passage

Because ACT Science passages contain so much information and you're skimming through them quickly, it's extremely important to not misread part of them. You might miss key information, misunderstand a fact, confuse two different ideas, etc. This can happen in any passage, even if it's about a topic you feel comfortable with. In the above passage, there are dozens of ways you could misread it, including confusing what happened in each experiment, confusing the various solutions that were mixed together, and confusing what temperature different steps and experiments occurred at.

If you're misreading passages consistently, alter how you're skimming or reading through the passages. If may help if you read the passage a bit more slowly, underline important parts, take notes in the margins, or even skip the passage altogether and go straight to the questions, only reading the passage to find a specific fact needed to answer a question. Reread Chapter 7 for additional strategies.

Practice is key here, and for whichever method you decide to use, be sure you try it out several times on practice sections before using it on exam day to ensure you don't get confused or run out of time using your new method.

#5: Not Knowing a Science Fact

Sometimes all it takes is not knowing a particular scientific fact to get a question wrong. This can happen even if you understand the rest of the passage and visuals perfectly. Take a look at this example:

Which of the following statements best explains why Study 1 did not yield the results the scientists expected?

A: Transcription only occurs in the nuclei of cells and is done to create DNA

B: Transcription only occurs in the nuclei of cells and is done to create mRNA

C: Transcription only occurs in the cytosol and is done to create DNA

D: Transcription only occurs in the cytosol and is done to create mRNA

No matter how much of the passage and the visuals you understand, you won't get this question right unless you remember that transcription occurs in the nuclei of cells and makes mRNA (answer B).

In Chapter 6 we went over every scientific fact you needed to know for ACT Science. There aren't that many, especially compared to most of the science tests you take in school, so make sure you have this information memorized!

#6: Making a Calculation Error

You won't be making calculations in ACT Science nearly as much as you will in the math section, but there are still numerous chances to make calculation errors. These mistakes will typically occur when you're answering calculations and estimates questions in Data Representation passages.

The majority of the calculations you need to do in ACT Science will only be basic arithmetic, but you aren't allowed a calculator on this section so it's easy to make small calculation errors if you're used to relying on your calculator a lot.

Here's an example:

Distance to Nearest Body of Water (m)	Soil Porosity (%)
50	31
60	33
70	37
80	41
90	45
100	47

Based on the results of Experiment 2, if the distance from the center of a 50m x 50m plot was 85m from the nearest body of water, the expected soil porosity at the plot would be closest to which of the following values?

A: 45%

B: 49%

C: 43%

D: 41%

The question wants to know soil porosity for a plot that's 85 m from the nearest body of water, but 85 m isn't included in the table. This means we'll need to do some interpolation. Both 80 m and 90 m are included in the table, and since 85 m is equidistant from those two points, we can simply find the average soil porosity of those two points to estimate the porosity at 85 m.

The calculation for this is: (Sum of the values)/(Number of values)

= (45 + 41)/2
= 86/2
=43

The correct answer is C, 43%, but there are many calculation errors one could make when solving this problem, such as adding incorrect numbers, subtracting instead of adding, dividing by the incorrect number, etc.

Practice is the best way to eliminate this type of error, especially if it's caused by you not using a calculator often. Never use a calculator on ACT Science, even for practice questions, or else you may become too dependent on it. It may also help to work out calculations for some of your math and science school work problems by hand to get additional practice.

#7: Making a Careless Error

Careless errors can be made on any question. You could misread a minor detail in the question, passage or answer choices. You could miss a question with a "NOT" or "EXCEPT." You could confuse two facts or viewpoints in your head and get the question wrong that way. You could even understand the question perfectly, do all the steps correctly, and then bubble in the wrong answer by mistake.

We discuss in-depth how to minimize careless errors in Chapter 11, but in general you should slow down a bit so you feel less rushed, make sure you read the question and answer choices correctly, and make sure you bubble in the correct answer. Spending a few extra seconds on a question is well worth it to make sure you don't make a silly mistake. If you find yourself continuously making careless errors, answer some practice problems/practice sections untimed so you can take as much time as you need to complete the questions, and see if that helps. Most careless mistakes are due to rushing to finish the section in time. If that's the case, keep completing practice science sections, slowly decreasing the amount of time you give yourself to finish, until you're finishing within the 35 minute official time frame.

#8: Not Understanding a Viewpoint

This mistake occurs on understanding viewpoints questions in Conflicting Viewpoints passages. It happens when you don't understand all or part of a particular scientist's or student's viewpoint, then answer questions incorrectly because of that.

Take this example passage and question:

Experiments

The students proposed 3 experiments using a Cycas revoluta population in an area with sap beetles and in which the percentage of ovule pollination in normally 99% (see table).

Experiment	Procedure
1	Some female *Cycas revoluta* cones are covered with plastic bags that exclude insects and wind.
2	Some female *Cycas revoluta* cones are covered with mesh bags that exclude insects, but not wind.
3	Some female *Cycas revoluta* cones are covered with cylinders that exclude wind, but not insects.

Student 1

In Cycas revoluta, 80% of ovule pollination results from insect pollination, and 20% results from wind pollination. These are the only two pollination mechanisms.

Cycas revoluta have mutually beneficial relationships with certain species of insects. Sap beetles swarm male Cycas revoluta cones when these cones are releasing pollen. When they enter the cones, the sap beetles become covered with the plant's pollen. The sap beetles then visit the female Cycas revoluta cones and deposit some of the pollen when it rubs off them. In the absence of sap beetles, the percent of ovule pollination in Cycas revoluta is about 20%.

Wind pollination is infrequent because Cycas revoluta pollen is large and heavy, making it difficult for it to travel long distances by wind. Additionally, the openings in the female cones are aligned horizontally, so wind-borne pollen must be blown horizontally in order to enter these cones.

Student 2

Wind pollination causes the majority, about 90%, of Cycas revoluta pollination, while only about 10% of ovule pollination in Cycas revoluta is caused by insects. Without wind pollination, the percent of ovule pollination decreases by 90%. If neither of these processes occur, the percent of ovule pollination decreases by 100%.

Wind tunnel experiments show that the shape of the female Cycas revoluta cones creates air currents that facilitate the horizontal movement of pollen into these cones so it is easier for windborne pollen to enter. Additionally, male Cycas revoluta cones produce enormous quantities of pollen, a trait that is common only in wind-pollinated plants. This means the majority of pollen can miss the female cones and the cones will still be pollinated because so much pollen is carried by the wind.

Pollination by sap beetles is infrequent because the beetles prefer other plant species over Cycas revoluta and only rarely visit Cycas revoluta, minimizing the amount of pollination they can perform.

Suppose the three experiments were performed as described. Student 2's hypothesis would be best supported if the percentages of ovule pollination were the roughly the same for which of the following two groups of female Cycas revoluta cones?

A: Those in Experiment 1 that were covered with plastic bags and those in Experiment 1 that were not covered with plastic bags.

B: Those in Experiment 1 that were covered with plastic bags and those in Experiment 2 that were covered with mesh bags.

C: Those in Experiment 2 that were covered with mesh bags and those in Experiment 2 that were not covered with mesh bags.

D: Those in Experiment 2 that were covered with mesh bags and those in Experiment 3 that were covered with cylinders.

From the passage, we can see that Student 2 believes that wind and insects are the only methods of pollination for Cycas revoluta and that wind accounts for the majority of the pollination. From the table, we also know that placing plastic bags over the cones prevents both wind and insect pollination, mesh bags prevent insect pollination, and cylinders prevent wind pollination.

This is all straightforward information, and if you had plenty of time and no pressure, you'd probably be able to figure out that C is the correct answer pretty easily (see Chapter 10 for an in-depth look at how to solve the problem). However, when you're taking the real ACT, you'll be under plenty of pressure, and it can be easy to get confused or just not understand what a particular viewpoint is or how it relates to a question.

If you struggle with understanding viewpoints, try taking more notes when reading through the Conflicting Viewpoints passage. This could include circling or underlining key phrases and/or making notes in the margins. For example, for this passage, you could write next to the table: plastic bags = no wind and insect pollination, mesh bags = no insect pollination, cylinders = no wind pollination. For Student 2, you could just write "wind pollination" to remind you that this student thinks the majority of Cycas revoluta pollination is due to wind. Brief notes like these only take a few seconds, but they can help you understand the main ideas of viewpoints.

#9: Not Understanding How Viewpoints Are Related

For comparing viewpoints questions, you'll be asked questions on how two or more viewpoints in a Conflicting Viewpoints passage are similar or different. Because you'll now be analyzing multiple viewpoints, there are now more chances to get confused and make a mistake.

Here's a sample question:

Based on the experiments described in the table, Students 1 and 2 would most likely agree that the percent of ovule pollination would be highest in female Cycas revoluta cones that are:

A: covered with plastic bags that block wind and insects

B: not covered with a bag or cylinder

C: covered with mesh bags that block insects

D: covered with cylinders that block wind

To answer this question, we need to know both Student 1's and Student 2's opinions so we can figure out which answer choice they would agree on. Student 1 believes the majority of Cycas revoluta pollination is from insects, and Student 2 believes it's from wind, but both agree wind and insects are the only methods of pollination for this plant species. That means B is correct since it allows both types of pollination to occur.

If you're struggling with these questions, follow the same guidelines above for reason #8, taking notes on each opinion the passage mentions. You can also reread Chapter 10 for a more in-depth look at how to tackle Conflicting Viewpoints passages.

The Best Way to Avoid ACT Science Mistakes

You may have noticed that many of these problems have the same solution: work through more practice problems and take careful note of where you're making mistakes. We've mentioned throughout this book how important practice questions are; they're the only way you can really get a feel for what ACT Science will be like and which question types you need to practice more.

Additionally, it can help to answer problems with no time restraints at first to get used to solving them without any time pressure, then gradually begin answering questions faster until you can solve them in 52 seconds or less.

Made in the USA
San Bernardino, CA
29 December 2019